THE ETHICS
OF READING

Previously Published Wellek Library Lectures

J. Hillis Miller

The Ethics
of Reading

KANT, de MAN,
ELIOT, TROLLOPE,
JAMES, and BENJAMIN

The Wellek Library Lectures
at the University of California, Irvine

Columbia University Press   New York

Columbia University Press
New York   Oxford
Copyright © 1987 Columbia University Press

Printed in the United States of America

∞
Library of Congress Cataloging-in-Publication Data

Miller, J. Hillis (Joseph Hillis), 1928–
   The ethics of reading.

   Bibliography: p.
   Includes index.
   1. Deconstruction.
2. Literature and Morals. I. Title.
PN98.R38M55   1986   801'.95   86-11708
ISBN 0-231-06334-2
ISBN 0-231-06335-0 (pbk.)

c 10 9 8 7 6 5 4 3 2 1
p 10 9 8 7 6 5 4 3 2 1

For Harold Bloom

Editorial Note

The Wellek Library Lectures are given annually at the University of California, Irvine, under the auspices of the Focused Research Program in Critical Theory and with the support of the Graduate Division. They are published in conjunction with the Irvine Studies in the Humanities, which is under the general editorship of Robert Folkenflik.

Focused Research Program in Critical Theory
David Carroll, Director

Contents

Preface

A preliminary version of this book was presented in May of 1985 as the Wellek Library Lectures at the University of California, Irvine. I am grateful for the honor of being part of this series. I thank my colleagues there for their many courtesies and especially thank Murray Krieger for serving so courteously as primary host. I am grateful also for the challenging comments made in discussions after my lectures. They have much helped me in revision. Though I did not know it then, my readings were inaugural, as I claim all true reading is. In this case the act of reading was the beginning of what I hope will be a permanent residence at Irvine, not as an outsider (dare I say "parasite"?), but as an insider, someone who may in his own turn play the role of the critic as host.

"Nein," sagte der Geistliche, "man muß nicht alles für wahr halten, man muß es nur für notwendig halten." "Trübselige Meinung," sagte K. "Die Lüge wird zur Weltordnung gemacht."
K. sagte das abschließend, aber sein Endurteil war es nicht. Er war zu müde, um alle Folgerungen der Geschichte übersehen zu können, es waren auch ungewohnte Gedankengänge, in die sie ihn führte, unwirkliche Dinge . . .

"No," said the priest, "it is not necessary to accept everything as true, one must only accept it as necessary." "A melancholy conclusion," said K. "It turns lying into a universal principle."
K. said that with finality, but it was not his final judgment. He was too tired to survey all the conclusions arising from the story, and the trains of thought into which it was leading him were unfamiliar, dealing with impalpabilities . . .

Franz Kafka, *Der Prozeß (The Trial)*

I lie awake night after night
And never get the answers right.
Did that play of mine send out
Certain men the English shot?
Did words of mine put too great strain
On that woman's reeling brain?
Could my spoken words have checked
That whereby a house lay wrecked?

W. B. Yeats, "The Man and the Echo"

THE ETHICS
OF READING

CHAPTER ONE

Reading Doing Reading

What could this mean, the ethics of reading? Is it not a solecism, a somewhat misleading way of saying "reading books for their ethical content or import"? What is the force of the genitive *of* in my title? Which way does it go? Does it mean a mode of ethics or of ethical action generated by reading, deriving from it, or does it mean an ethics intrinsic to reading, remaining within it? Or does the *of* in this case go both ways at once? In what sense can or should the act of reading be itself ethical or have an ethical import? Should not reading be thought of as primarily cognitive, as a matter of understanding what is said, after which some ethical use of that reading might or might not be made, but in any case as something extraneous to the primary act of reading as such?

I propose to argue, in the face of such assumptions, that there is a necessary ethical moment in that act of reading as such, a moment neither cognitive, nor political, nor social, nor interpersonal, but properly and independently ethical. I shall explore this by way of the reading of a number of passages, first in chapters reading examples from a philosopher and a literary theorist to sketch out the ground of the topic, and then in three novelists, George Eliot, Anthony Trollope, and Henry James, one chapter for each. In the chapters on the novelists I shall concentrate on texts in which the novelists read themselves, taking that act of self-reading as paradigmatic for reading in general, or at least as offering records of salient examples of reading. I reserve for a later book investigation of my topic through reading of works of fiction themselves. In principle the ethics of reading could be explored by way of examples chosen from poetry, from philosophy, even from political texts or essays in literary criticism. The choice of work by novelists is therefore to some extent arbitrary, though of course it will determine the strategy of the argument, for example the investigation of a possible analogy between the ethical choices of characters within novels and the ethical acts of readers of novels. That is one version of the double genitive in "ethics *of* reading." Does the ethical act *of* the protagonist inside the book correspond to the ethical acts the reading of the book generates outside the book?

I shall argue, however, that there is a peculiar and unexpected relation between the affirmation of universal moral law and storytelling. It would seem that such a law would stand by itself and that its connection either to narration as such or to any particular narrative would be adventitious and superficial at best. Nevertheless, as I shall show, the moral law gives rise by an intrinsic necessity to storytelling, even if that storytelling in one way or another puts in question or subverts the moral law. Ethics and narration cannot be kept separate, though their relation is neither symmetrical nor harmonious. Moreover, the stories that confrontation of the moral law generates are precisely versions of that kind of teleological, reasonable, and lawfully determined narration we call history.

It may be seen from my use of examples that I think my topic is one that cannot be adequately discussed in the abstract. It *must* be analyzed and demonstrated in terms of specific cases. The relation between examples and conceptual generalizations about the ethics of reading is in fact one of the problematic areas in any theory of the ethics of reading. It is easy to see that no choice of examples is innocent. It is a somewhat arbitrary selection for which the chooser must take responsibility. On the other hand, there is no doing, in this region of the conduct of life, without examples.

This is as true of philosophical treatises on ethics as it is of literary study, as I shall demonstrate by means of an example from Kant in my second chapter here. Without storytelling there is no theory of ethics. Narratives, examples, stories, such as Kant's little story of the man who makes a promise intending not to keep it, are indispensable to thinking about ethics. An understanding of ethics as a region of philosophical or conceptual investigation depends, perhaps surprisingly, on mastery of the ability to interpret written stories, that is, on a kind of mastery usually thought to be the province of the literary critic. If this is true it has important implications for my topic of the ethics of reading, as well as for my claim that the rhetorical study of literature has crucial practical implications for our moral, social, and political lives. I have said that there is a special appropriateness of narrative examples for an investigation of the ethics of reading, but the reasons for this must not be misunderstood. It is not because stories contain the thematic dramatization of ethical situations, choices, and judgments that they are especially appropriate for my topic, but for a reverse reason, that is, because ethics itself has a peculiar relation to that form of language we call narrative. The thematic dramatizations of ethical topics in narratives are the oblique allegorization of this linguistic necessity. On this difficult point I shall have more to say later.

Even in the relatively spacious enclosure of six chapters only a beginning can be made with my topic. I claim that it is of fundamental importance for literary and humanistic study today. The stakes are large in getting it right, and there is a corresponding danger of getting it wrong, perhaps through fatigue or boredom or anxiety, or as a result of some other weakness preventing one from keeping one's mind on the topic, in place, so to speak. The attractions of inattention are immense, and we are likely to be, like Joseph K. in my epigraph, too tired to follow out all the pathways of thought into which a given story leads. Or we may be prone, like K. in *The Castle,* to fall asleep just when we are at last about to have a chance to confront the authority who might clarify everything. Reading itself is extraordinarily hard work. It does not occur all that often. Clearheaded reflection on what really happens in an act of reading is even more difficult and rare. It is an event traces of which are found here and there in written form, like those tracks left in a bubble-chamber by the passage of a particle from outer space. The passages I propose to discuss here are such traces or tracks.

What do I mean by the ethical? And what do I claim is gained by shifting the ground from the much more common, in fact almost universal, topic of literary study these days, namely investigations of the political, historical, and social connections of literature? To speak of the ethics of reading rather than, for example, of the "politics of interpretation"[1] returns from an area of investigation which is likely to be vague and speculative, often unhelpfully polemical, to something that has at least a chance to be concrete, namely the real situation of a man or woman reading a book, teaching a class, writing a critical essay. No doubt that "situation" spreads out to involve institutional, historical, economic, and political "contexts," but it begins with and returns to the man or woman face to face with the words on the page. My question is whether ethical decision or responsibility is in any way necessarily involved in that situation and act of reading, and if so, how and of what kind, responsibility to whom or to what, decision to do what?

The ethical moment in the act of reading, then, if there is one, faces in two directions. On the one hand it is a response to something, responsible to it, responsive to it, respectful of it. In any ethical moment there is an imperative, some "I must" or *Ich kann nicht anders*. I *must* do this. I cannot do otherwise. If the response is not one of necessity, grounded in some "must," if it is a freedom to do what one likes, for example to make a literary text mean what one likes, then it is not ethical, as when we say, "That isn't ethical." On the other hand, the ethical moment in reading leads to an act. It enters into the social, institutional, political realms, for example in what the teacher says to the class or in what the critic writes. No doubt the political and the ethical are always intimately intertwined, but an ethical act that is fully determined by political considerations or responsibilities is no longer ethical. It could even in a certain sense be said to be amoral. The same thing could be said of cases in which the apparently ethical is subordinated to the epistemological, to some act of cognition. If there is to be such a thing as an ethical moment in the act of reading, teaching, or writing about literature, it must be sui generis, something individual and particular, itself a source of political or cognitive acts, not subordinated to them. The flow of power must not be all in one direction. There must be an influx of performative power from the linguistic transactions involved in the act of reading into the realms of knowledge, politics, and history. Literature must be in some way a cause and not merely an effect, if the study of literature is to be other than the relatively trivial study of one of the epiphenomena of society, part of the technological assimilation or assertion of mastery over all features of human life which is called "the human sciences." How this can be, and the somewhat unsettling implications of this "how," my passages and examples will show.

    Let me specify what I mean by saying the attempt to explain works of literature by their political, social, and historical contexts is likely to be "vague and speculative." The commitment to this as a main focus of literary study, perhaps *the* main responsibility of literary study, is so widespread today, as a project if not all that often as a fulfilled intention, that it will be helpful, even imperative, to distinguish my project at the outset from this other one. It is not difficult to understand some of the complex motives that have led to this massive shift in the orientation of literary studies. It may be partly that ennui and fatigue I mentioned above. It is so hard, too hard, to keep one's attention on the text. It may be partly a sense of guilt in occupying oneself with something so trivial, so disconnected from "life" and "reality," as novels and poems, in comparison with the serious business of history, politics, and the class struggle. It may be fear of literature, an aversion of the eyes from some anarchic power that is felt in it and that one would like to tame, control, or repress. One motive for the study of the historical and social connections of literature is the lure of intellectual mastery promised by all such hermeneutical theories of meaning, whether they are social and historical, as in the case of

Marxist criticism, or are religious or psychological, as in Gadamerian hermeneutics and psychoanalytic hermeneutics respectively. By "hermeneutical" I mean the measuring and ascertaining of the meaning of a text by something nontextual outside that text: God or some other transcendent power, society, history, economic conditions, the psychology of the author, the "original" of the text in "real life."

The social, political, and historical "backgrounds" or "contexts" of a given work may indeed be studied in detail and specified with exactitude, though the amount of hard empirical research necessary to do this is often underestimated by literary critics who say they want to study the historical and political dimensions of literature. The vagueness and ungrounded speculation, the unexamined *a prioris,* begin just at that place where the relation between the "background" or "context" and the literary text as such, the words on the page, is asserted. The social, historical, or political conditions are said to be the "cause" or the "determining context" of the work, or the work is said to "mirror" its background, or the work is said to be "penetrated" or "permeated" by the social and class assumptions of its author or his milieu, or the work is said to express the "ideology" of its author's class and historical moment and by way of that ideology to express obliquely the "real historical and social conditions" of that time, place, and class. As I have elsewhere argued,[2] each of these relations is in fact one figure of speech or another. Mirroring, reflection, or mimesis is a species of metaphor. It assumes a similarity between the reflection and what is reflected. The notion of context hovers uneasily between metonymy in the sense of mere contingent adjacency and synecdoche, part for whole, with an assumption that the part is some way genuinely like the whole. The notion of penetration or permeation is an example of that form of figure called anastomosis, the insertion of a word within another word, as in the example Joyce gives, "underdarkneath," or as in the expression of this notion of the relation of language to the political and social realms Bakhtin gives in *Marxism and the Philosophy of Language:* "Languages are philosophies—not abstract but concrete social philosophies, penetrated by a system of values inseparable from living practice and class struggle."[3] Ideology, finally, is a species of anamorphosis, the transformation of one form into another which is recognizable as being a distortion of its original only when viewed from a certain angle.

All of these models belong to the problematic of inside outside polarities, open to a variety of crossings, displacements, and substitutions, as inside becomes outside, outside inside, or as features on either side cross over the wall, membrane, or partition dividing the sides. Understanding such displacements, substitutions, and crossings requires a linguistic or rhetorical analysis, a mastery of the varieties of figure inhabiting this region of linguistic transaction. Interpretation of these figures of crossing hovers uneasily around the exceedingly difficult problem of how something apparently non-linguistic, social power or force, material means of production, distribution, and consumption, passes over the border into the linguistic. How does the apparently nonlinguistic become language, or, on the other hand, how does language cross over to the nonlinguistic and, as Paul de Man puts it, "generate" "the materiality of actual history"?[4] Each of these four models, then, and each of the innumerable variants of them that can be identified, requires a vigilant and sophisticated rhetorical analysis. This is another way of saying that the study of literature, even the study of the historical and social relations or determinants of literature, remains within the study of language.

Moreover, even when the exact form of the relation of the text to its context has been identified, the work of interpretation has only begun. The difficult business of actually reading the work and showing how the adduced historical context inheres in the fine grain of its language still remains to be done. Until it is done nothing has been done beyond making a vague claim that the context "explains" the text. Nothing is more urgently needed these days in humanistic study than the incorporation of the rhetorical study of literature into the study of the historical, social, and ideological dimensions of literature. Only such an incorporation would complicate or contest the one way flow from history to work which is assumed in one way or another by each of the four models

described above, though the "incorporation" may well be destined
to be the entry of a parasitical virus within the host cell, interfering
with the working of that cell and reprogramming it in unforeseen
ways. In one way or another, according to each of these models,
the work of literature is said to be the reflection or example of
social, historical, and ideological forces at a given time and place.
A given novel, for example, is entirely to be accounted for and is
accountable to forces, powers, surveillances coming from outside
itself. It expresses, in spite of itself, an ideology. No corner is left
anywhere for deviation, idiosyncrasy, freedom, or performative power.
Literature in no sense makes history but is made by it, since the
determining forces of history are material means of production,
distribution, and consumption. The latter create certain class ideologies, which are in turn reflected in works of literature. There is
not any margin or deviation left over which cannot be accounted
for by those strategies of anamorphosic interpretation I mentioned
above. If this view of literature were true, it would make the study
of literature a somewhat dreary business, since what would be found
in literature would be what is already known by the interpreter and
what can more clearly be known and seen elsewhere, for example
by the study of history and society as such. The study of literature
would then be no more than the study of a symptom or super-
structure of something else more real and more important, and
literature would be no more than a minor by-product of history,
not something that in any way makes history.

      It is this assumption that I want to contest by shifting
to a focus on the question of the ethical moment in writing or
narrating novels, acting as a character within them, reading novels,
writing about them. In what I call "the ethical moment" there is
a claim made on the author writing the work, on the narrator telling
the story within the fiction of the novel, on the characters within
the story at decisive moments of their lives, and on the reader,
teacher, or critic responding to the work. This ethical "I must"
cannot, I propose to show, be accounted for by the social and
historical forces that impinge upon it. In fact the ethical moment
contests these forces or is subversive of them. The ethical moment,

in all four of its dimensions, is genuinely productive and inaugural in its effects on history, though in ways that are by no means reassuring or predictably benign, as my examples will show. My assumption, moreover, is that there are analogies among all four of these ethical moments, that of the author, the narrator, the character, and the reader, teacher, critic, though what is the basis of these analogies, what *logos* controls them, remains to be interrogated.[5]

I have yet another motive for choosing what I call "the ethics of reading" for my topic. The attacks on the sort of rhetorical analysis of works of literature I and some others try to do, attacks, that is, on so-called "deconstruction," from *Newsweek* all the way up or down to those wielding a different sort of authority, such as Walter Jackson Bate or René Wellek,[6] focus on the presumed negativity or "nihilism" of this mode of criticism. The word "nihilism" is used in such polemics loosely, to say the least, and in a way quite false to its proper meaning as used, for example, by Nietzsche and Heidegger. As the latter persuasively argue, "nihilism" is a name for a reflex of metaphysics that remains entirely within the assumptions of metaphysics.[7] One facet of the misuse of the term nihilism as a bad label for deconstruction is the assertion that deconstruction removes all grounds of certainty or authority in literary interpretation. Deconstruction, such (mis)readers of it claim, asserts that the reader, teacher, or critic is free to make the text mean anything he wants it to mean. The implicit or explicit reproach is that this is immoral because it annihilates the traditional use of the great texts of our culture from Homer and the Bible on down as the foundation and embodiment, the means of preserving and transmitting, the basic humanistic values of our culture. I want to demonstrate that this line of thought, whether expressed in the mass media or in academic circles, is a mistake. It is a misreading of the work of the deconstructive critics. Beyond that, it is a basic misunderstanding of the way the ethical moment enters into the act of reading, teaching, or writing criticism. That moment is not a matter of response to a thematic content asserting this or that idea about morality. It is a much more fundamental "I must"

responding to the language of literature in itself, as I shall try to
show.

Deconstruction is nothing more or less than good reading
as such. Such attacks on it as I have mentioned make a triple
mistake. They misread the plain sense of what Derrida or de Man,
for example, say about the relation of reader to text. Neither has
ever asserted the freedom of the reader to make the text mean
anything he or she wants it to mean. Each has in fact asserted the
reverse. Second, such attacks misuse the term nihilism, misunder-
stand its relation to the ethical, and misapply it in any case in using
it as a label for deconstruction. It is rather the attackers who are
themselves a manifestation of nihilism in the strict historical meaning
of that word. Such attacks, finally, are based on a misunderstanding
of the ethical moment in reading. This book is written in part as
a response to this triple misunderstanding. It is an attempt at least
to clarify the issues. As I said, the stakes are large in getting the
ethics of reading right, with a corresponding danger of getting it
wrong.

In my attempt to get it right I shall turn now to my
examples of authors reading their own work, first to Kant, then in
the following chapters to the others. This procedure, it should be
noted at the outset, reproduces the problems it is apparently meant
to solve. I shall be trying to perform several acts of reading myself.
It might well be asked what my own ethical responsibilities are in
these acts of reading. Do these readings have ethical import in the
way I claim genuine readings must, and, if so, for whom? Are my
readings "events" themselves or only the registering of events that
have taken place elsewhere, for example when the passages were
written? Can such events or acts of reading be repeated, and are
they the same when they are repeated? Finally, my passages raise
the question of exemplarity, of the relation of the particular to the
general which is in itself a central question in any ethical theory
and consequently also in any theory of the ethics of reading. As a
reader, so it seems, I should above all have respect for the text,
not deviate by one iota in my report of the text from what it says.
The letter of the text must become my law when I read it. But is

that respect for the text a respect for its unique particularity or for the way it is an example of a more universal law? Do all my passages say "the same thing" about the ethical moment in reading or have the same implications for a theory of the ethics of reading, or are they incommensurate? That is analogous to the question I raised earlier about the analogies between the situations of writer, narrator, character within the story and, on the other hand, the situations of reader, teacher, or critic. Do my novelists all say "the same thing" on this topic or make the same thing happen when we read them? If all are analogous, what is the base of the analogy, what is its law? What difference would it make if we said they mean the same or do the same or, on the other hand, if we denied that?

The choice of examples, moreover, and their ordering, is never innocent. Does not my choice of examples load the dice, predetermine the conclusions I can reach and, like all examples, in fact form the essence of the argument it is apparently only meant to exemplify? It is all very well for me to claim that the order of my examples (from Kant to de Man to Eliot to Trollope to James and Benjamin) is arbitrary, that other examples might have been chosen, or that these examples put in a different order would have justified the same conclusions. Does not the order of the examples, whatever I say, magically generate a narrative and seem to tell a story with beginning, middle, and end, a logic and teleology of its own? What comes after presupposes what came before and seems "deeper in" or "further along" toward some conclusion, so ingrained is the habit of narrative and its cognitive implications. These questions are in one way or another at issue in all of my examples. To those I now turn to see if they will take us into closer proximity to the law governing the ethics of reading. For which of us would want to remain outside that law, exterior to it, an outlaw?

CHAPTER TWO

Reading Telling: Kant

My first example is from Immanuel Kant's *Grundlegung zur Metaphysik der Sitten (Foundations of the Metaphysics of Morals)* (1785). Already that choice involves a complex set of moves or placements, even "political" commitments, if not ethical choices, in the sense that we speak of "academic politics." To put all I have to say under the aegis of Kant by choosing to speak of him first, as though all I have to say might flow from what I have to say about him, or from what he said himself, is so far from innocent that it involves me in a whole set of complicities at once, whether I wish them or not, am aware of them or not, complicities which it might require a more or less interminable analysis to untangle.

To choose Kant, so it seems, is to commit oneself at the outset to a certain theory of ethics among others, one that is voluntarist and subjectivistic, but at the same time reaffirms the category of duty and those highest values of renunciation and disinterested service which are inherited from Stoicism, on the one hand, but are on the other hand inseparable from Christianity and especially important in Protestantism. In spite of Kant's pretense of magisterial objectivity and universality he ends up reaffirming just the morality of his country, class, religion, and time. This comedy is nowhere more likely to be played out than in ethical theory.

Under the guise of universal truth, it can be argued, Kant is doing no more than reaffirming the presuppositions, the ideology, of a certain class, religion, time in history, and place in Europe. To invoke Kant today, it might appear, is to beg all the questions that ought to remain questions.

To choose Kant, but Kant's ethics rather than his epistemology in the *Critique of Pure Reason* or his aesthetics in the *Critique of Judgment,* is both to situate oneself within the lively current debates about Kant[1] and at the same time to put oneself apparently at the periphery of those debates, outside of where the action is, though, as my note shows, there is also a lively current interest in Kant's writings on ethics. The latter does not, however, take place for the most part within literary study as such.

To choose Kant, in any case, is to place oneself, willynilly, within a complex history of the reception of Kant. This history has for an American student of literature writing today at least a double line. On the one hand there is the immense diffuse importance Kant has had, partly by way of his misinterpretation by Schiller, on the development of theories of literature and on the creation of the institutionalized study of literature and the humanities generally in England and the United States. An American writing today writes from within that heritage, whether he knows it or not, as witness, for example, the invocation of Kant at crucial moments in the polemics of both René Wellek and Walter Jackson Bate against "deconstruction" for "destroying literary studies" and helping to precipitate and greatly exacerbate a "crisis in English studies" (see note 1). On the other hand, Kant enters in a complex way into the history since Kant's time of European philosophy. This includes of course all three of his main topics, epistemology and aesthetics as well as ethics.

The names of Nietzsche, Heidegger, and Freud will schematize three main moments in the response to Kant as a theorist of ethics. Each of these has in a different way fundamentally challenged Kant's claim to have established universal foundations of the metaphysics of morals, foundations valid for all times and places. It would be exceedingly naive to write about Kant without awareness of this after-history, which is our own history, for example without taking into account the challenge posed to Kant's theories of freedom and subjectivity by Freud's concept of the unconscious, or by Nietzsche's constant polemic against Kant, for example in *The Genealogy of Morals* (though Nietzsche is more dependent on Kant than he is willing to admit), or by Heidegger's situating of the definition of man as subjectivity and will as a climactic moment in the history of metaphysics, that is, the history in some sense of an error induced by the occultation of Being. All this extremely dense, complex, and thick history stands between us and Kant like an opaque mist or like an impenetrable thicket of thorns around the sleeping beauty, forbidding direct access to Kant. Nevertheless, let us look at a crucial passage in Kant's *Grundlegung,* to try to see just what it says and what is problematic about what it says, keeping in mind that my interest is not in ethics as such but in the ethics of reading and in the relation of the ethical moment in reading to relation in the sense of giving an account, telling a story, narrating.

The passage is a footnote in which Kant defends his use of the term "respect" (Achtung). Footnotes, as any astute reader will know, are often places where an author gives himself away in one way or another in the act of fabricating a protective cover. A footnote often reveals an uneasiness, identifies a fissure or seam in an author's thought by saying it is not there. Kant's footnote is no exception. This footnote says a mouthful, as they say. Moreover, it is an example of that sort of passage which, for reasons of strategy and economy, I have chosen to concentrate on in this book, namely passages where an author reads himself. In such passages the ethics of reading is manifested in one of its most revealing versions, that is, in places where the author and the reader are the same. At such moments an author turns back on himself, so to speak, turns back on a text he or she has written, re-reads it, and, it may be, performs an act which can be called an example of the ethics of reading. My examples from de Man, George Eliot, Trollope, and James are all of this sort, as is this footnote by Kant. A footnote, as in this case, is often a commentary on the main text, a reading of it, with all the possibilities of alteration, suppression, inadvertent revelation, or irrelevance which characterize "readings" by a third party, you or I, for example, as readers of Kant.

Kant has been explaining that "Duty is the necessity of an action executed from respect for law" (Pflicht ist die Notwendigkeit einer Handlung aus Achtung fürs Gesetz).[2] This means that a moral action must not be performed either from "inclination" (Neigung), that is, because I want to do it, am attracted by something outside myself, nor from calculation of its results, even good ones for myself or for others. When these private and social motives are removed, "nothing remains which can determine the will objectively except the law [das Gesetz], and nothing subjectively except pure respect [reine Achtung] for this practical law." Readers of Kant will know the importance of this notion of purity. It means the removal of everything contingent, empirical, local, such as the moral codes of a particular time, place, class, country, or culture, in order to leave the absolutely universal, abstracted from all particularity. What Kant calls "the highest and unconditional good" can only be found in the pure will of a rational being directed out of respect toward what he calls the "law in itself" (Gesetz an sich selbst) (E, 20; G, 27), the "law as such" (Gesetzmäßigkeit) (E, 21; G, 28), whatever *that* means. This is just what is most in question here and for the ethics of reading "in general."

At this point Kant draws himself up and inserts a footnote attempting to clarify what he means by *Achtung* and distinguishing it from any sort of subjective feeling. Though *Achtung* would have been the ordinary eighteenth-century German word for "respect," and though the word did not apparently carry the military connotations it has today, nevertheless its nuances were not quite the same as the English word *respect*. *Achtung* means "attention, heed," as well as "esteem, respect, regard." It suggests a coerced or alarmed taking notice of something possibly dangerous. The verb *achten* with "auf" means "pay attention or regard or heed to" as well as (without "auf") "esteem, respect, value, set store by, have regard for, have a high opinion of." *Achtung!,* now at least, means "look out! take care! beware!" In his footnote Kant wants to say that

Achtung in the sense he is using it to mean respect for the moral law as such is a feeling which is not a feeling, or not in the usual sense a feeling. It is easy to see that much hangs on persuading the reader to accept this distinction, since otherwise he or she might be led to believe that ethics is in one way or another the product of mere subjective feeling. Here is the entire footnote. If we can read it accurately in the context of its surrounding paragraphs in the main text we shall have at least a preliminary grasp of Kant's theory of ethics as well as of what is most problematic about that theory, what is unspoken or implicit in it. Whether my reading of this passage by Kant about respect is properly respectful, or does violence to the text, and whether my reading of Kant or my reader's reading of what I say are in any sense ethical acts I must leave it to the reader to judge:

> It might be objected that I take refuge in an obscure feeling [in einem dunkelen Gefühle] behind the word "respect," instead of clearly resolving the question with a concept of reason. But though respect is a feeling, it is not one received through any [outer] influence [kein durch Einfluß empfangenes] but is self-wrought by a rational concept [einen Vernunftbegriff selbstgewirktes Gefühl]: thus it differs specifically from all feelings of the former kind which may be referred to inclination or fear [Neigung oder Furcht]. What I recognize directly as a law for myself [als Gesetz für mich] I recognize with respect, which means merely the consciousness of the submission of my will to a law without the intervention of other influences on my mind. The direct determination of the will by the law and the consciousness of this determination is respect: thus respect can be regarded as the effect of the law on the subject and not as the cause of the law [nicht als Ursache desselben]. Respect is properly the conception of a worth which thwarts my self-love. Thus it is regarded as an object neither of inclination nor of fear, though it has something analogous to both [obgleich es mit beiden zugleich etwas Analogisches hat: the translation omits "zugleich," which means "at the same time, simultaneously," and hence hides the play on two words ending in "gleich," which means "like, analogous to," as a "Gleichnis" is a likeness; "obgleich," "zugleich," "Analogisches," words for likeness echo through the phrase as a kind of underthought or ground bass

emphasizing the problem Kant is raising]. The only object of respect is the law, and indeed only the law which we impose on ourselves and yet recognize as necessary in itself [das wir uns selbst und doch als an sich notwendig auferlegen]. As a law, we are subject to it without consulting self-love; as imposed on us by ourselves, it is a consequence of our will. In the former respect it is analogous to fear and in the latter to inclination. All respect for a person is only respect for the law [Alle Achtung für eine Person ist eigentlich nur Achtung fürs Gesetz] (of righteousness, etc.) of which the person provides an example [das Beispiel]. Because we see the improvement of our talents as a duty, we think of a person of talents as the example of a law, as it were [auch gleichsam das Beispiel eines Gesetzes vor] (the law that we should by practice become like him in his talents), and that constitutes our respect. All so-called moral interest consists solely in respect for the law. (E, 20–21; G, 27–28)

Is it possible, I ask first, to add another analogy to those Kant proposes and to say that our respect for a text is like our respect for a person, that is, it is respect not for the text in itself but respect for a law which the text exemplifies? Which would be the literal ground of this analogy, a text or a person, which the metaphor? What would it mean to say in this case that a text is like a person? My claim that reading this footnote by Kant will help understand the ethics of reading depends on presuming the validity of this analogy. Kant shows what it might mean to say that our response to a person is ethical, in the sense that we see him or her as an example of a transcendent and universal moral law. Is there any possibility that the law exemplified by a text might also be properly ethical, or have an ethical moment, as opposed to grammatical, syntactic, or tropological dimensions? I mean by an ethical moment not the thematic statement or dramatization of some ethical law ("Thou shalt not commit adultery," for example, surely a staple ethical theme of novels), but the effective and functional embodiment of some ethical law in action. If that were the case, the effect on the reader of the text would be like the effect on him of the moral law, that is, a categorical imperative, necessarily binding his will or leading him willingly to bind his own will. The act of reading would lead the reader voluntarily to impose the necessary ethical law embodied in that text on himself.

Accepting for the moment the possibility that respect for a text may be somehow analogous to respect for a person who is an example of the moral law, let me return to Kant's words, out of respect for the text of his footnote. The careful reader will have noted that Kant somewhat uneasily evades several dangers simultaneously with his carefully circumscribed definition of "respect." He does this, however, only to be vulnerable to another danger which remains at the end of the footnote still only implicit in what he says, as if it were generated by the act of protective circumscription. This danger becomes more explicit in the following paragraphs of the main text. If respect, as Kant affirms, is a feeling, it lacks one of the main characteristics of feelings for Kant, namely that feelings are generated as "inclination" or "fear," a tendency to approach or flee, in response to something external to the self. A feeling is a response to an "influence" (Einfluß) which flows into the mind from without, coercing it and generating its affects. Respect, however, is not a feeling in this sense. It is a feeling which is not a feeling. It is self-wrought rather than being a response to something external. It is not a movement toward or away from something desired or feared. On the other hand, respect is a response to something that preexists it and exists outside the mind, not the creation of that something. If Kant must avoid at all costs (at the cost of logical coherence) the possibility that *Achtung* is mere reflex reaction of desire or fear, in the other direction he must avoid at all costs the possibility that since respect is "self-wrought" it creates or projects its object, the moral law as such. Kant is like a man walking a knife-edge on a mountaintop, with an abyss on either side, the abyss of a productive spontaneity on the one side, the abyss of a passive receptivity on the other. The knife-edge, however, itself turns into an abyss, as I shall show.

If respect neither spontaneously creates its own object nor is a passive response to something outside itself that exists as a manifest objective power, what then is respect respect for or respectful of? What, exactly, is the law? How can I confront it, or define it, or have access to it? The reader would like to know, just as Kafka's man from the country, in the parable "Before the Law," respectfully requests a face-to-face confrontation with the law. Kant gives, and can give, only negative or indirect definitions of the moral law. The law is not, for example, any particular moral law that can be formulated as a maxim: "Don't tell lies"; "Thou shalt not steal"; "Thou shalt not commit adultery," etc. The law in question is the law as such. This means that the relation of any particular moral law that can be formulated in so many words to the law as such is something like, or is analogous to, the relation between a person we respect because he or she embodies the moral law and the law itself. "Mere conformity to the law as such," says Kant in the paragraph in the main text following the footnote, "(without as-suming any particular law applicable to certain actions) serves as the principle of the will" (Hier ist nun die bloße Gesetzmäßigkeit überhaupt [ohne irgend ein auf gewisse Handlungen bestimmtes Gesetz zum Grunde zu legen] das, was dem Willen zum Prinzip dient) (E, 21; G, 28); the translation misses the metaphor of ground-ing or establishing a solid base in the German phrase "zum Grunde zu legen," "to lay down as a ground."

What, then, is the law as such? The reader would like to know. He would like to have access to it, to confront it face to face, to see it written down somewhere, so he can know whether or not he is obeying it. Well, Kant cannot tell you exactly what the law as such is, in so many words, nor can he tell you exactly where it is, or where it comes from. The law, as Jacques Derrida puts it, gives itself without giving itself.[3] It may only be confronted in its delegates or representatives or by its effects on us or on others. It is those effects that generate respect for the law. But if Kant cannot tell you exactly what the law is, where it is, or where it comes from, he can nevertheless tell you to what it is analogous. Into the vacant place where there is no direct access to the law as such, but where we stand respectfully, like the countryman in Kafka's parable, "before the law," is displaced by metaphor or some other form of analogy two forms of feeling that *can* be grasped and named directly. Respect for the law is said to be analogous to just those two feelings which it has been said not to be: inclination and fear. The name for this procedure of naming by figures of speech what cannot be named literally because it cannot be faced directly is catachresis or, as Kant calls it in paragraph fifty-nine of the *Critique of Judgment,* "hypotyposis" (Hypotypose). Kant's linguistic procedure in this footnote is an example of the forced or abusive transfer of terms from an alien realm to name something which has no proper name in itself since it is not an object which can be directly confronted by the senses. That is what the word *catachresis* means; etymologically: "against usage." What is "forced or abusive" in this case is clear enough. Kant has said that respect for the law is not based on fear or inclination, but since there is no proper word for what it is based on, he is forced to say it is like just those two feelings, fear and inclination, he has said it is *not* like.

Respect for the law, says Kant, is like fear in that we recognize the law as necessary, unavoidable. In this the law is like, say, some natural catastrophe that we fear. The law is something we are subject to whether we like it or not. We accept the law, necessarily, without consulting that most basic of motives, self-love. Respect for the law, on the other hand, is also analogous to inclination in that we impose the law freely on ourselves. We really want to obey the law. In this sense respect for the law is like the inclination that leads us to desire something desirable. Not only do we really want to respect the law, but since the law is a law for ourselves, it is something we impose freely on ourselves as reasonable beings. In that sense respect for the law is respect for ourselves as being worthy of the law or worthy of having a law for ourselves, worthy of having a categorical imperative imposed on us. Or rather, since each act of respect for the law is unique and individual, a moment within historical time, so to speak, even though the law as such is universal and transhistorical, it would be better to stick to the first person singular and say, "I freely impose the moral law on myself, though at the same time I respect its absolute necessity. I freely impose the moral law on myself, as a law for myself, out of respect for the law, and in respecting the law I respect myself as a free rational self able to have respect for the law and able to act ethically on the basis of the law." In doing all this, if I can do it, in one complex single momentary movement of my will, I myself become an example of the moral law, an embodiment of it. As such I become worthy of the respect of others.

If I remember at this point the additional analogy I added to Kant's analogies and say that respect for a text is like respect for a person, can I say that this is because the creation of the text by the author is a response to the law, not in answer to any particular, specifiable moral law, such as the prohibition against adultery, but a response to the moral law as such? My examples will confirm that this is the case, both for the novels themselves in what they say when we read them and for what the novelists say about the conditions under which the novels were written. In this book the emphasis, because of limitations of space, will be on the latter, that is, on what the novelists say rather than on the novels themselves. If a philosophical, literary, or critical text is worthy of our respect it can only be because it has been created out of respect for the law, just as my respect is not for a person as such but for the person as an example of the law. Which way does this analogy go? Is the concept of a person perhaps covertly modeled on the concept of a text, or is a text worthy of our respect because it is like a person, or are both like one another because each is analogous to that third thing, spring and generative source of both, the law as such? It is easy to assume that the concept of the freely willing subjectivity, the self, ego, or "Ich," takes prec- edence here and is the fundamental presupposition of all Kant's thinking about ethics or the practical reason, but analogies have a way of working both ways. It may be that the concept of a person is to some degree or in some way modeled on that for which it is the model. Novels may be a place to see how this question of priority remains a question. The question is experienced concretely by the reader of a novel in the analogy he recognizes between the character in the novel as an example of the moral law and the text itself as an example of the moral law. My act of reading the character, understanding him, an act articulated in the novel by the narrator,

is an allegory of my act of reading the text, figuring it out, as they
say.

But is this analogy really justified in the case of Kant?
Am I not doing disrespectful violence to the passage in Kant I claim
to be reading by arguing that it can be used as the basis of a
theory of the ethics of reading novels? What does Kant's theory of
ethics have to do with narrative, with storytelling, or even with
history as the story we tell about the changes of society through
the centuries? The moral law as such is above and beyond all that.
It remains absolutely the same at all times and places and for all
persons. No person can be more than a contingent example of it.
No story, it would seem, can do other than falsify it by entangling
the law in the meshes of the extrinsic particulars of a time and
place, imaginary or real. In spite of that, and as if to give it the
lie, the reader can watch a shadowy narrative and the inadvertent
demonstration of the necessity of narrative in any account of ethics
slowly emerge as Kant develops his concept of respect. Even when
it is defined as pure practical reason, ethics involves narrative, as
its subversive accomplice. Storytelling is the impurity which is
necessary in any discourse about the moral law as such, in spite
of the law's austere indifference to persons, stories, and history.
There is no theory of ethics, no theory of the moral law and of
its irresistible, stringent imperative, its "Thou shalt" and "Thou
shalt not," without storytelling and the temporalization (in several
senses of the word) which is an intrinsic feature of all narrative.
This justifies, I claim, my choice of novels and stories to illustrate
the ethics of reading.

The reader has already encountered in the footnote itself
one narrative element. I have respect not for a person but for a
person as an example of some ethical value which is in turn an
example of the law as such. If I cannot confront the law directly,
stand face to face with it, so to speak (for reasons which are not
yet clear, perhaps will never be wholly clear), I can, on the other
hand, confront face to face a person who is an example of the law.
There is already a latent story in that confrontation. It implies the
story of their interaction or mutual influence or growing knowledge

of one another. If I know the person well enough to know that he is an example of the law, there must be a story to tell about our relation. It might be the basic story, for example, so fundamental to the novel as a genre, of the relation between the narrator and the protagonist whose story he tells as an example for himself and for the reader. The narrator can only know what the character knows. The narrator therefore, it may be, has access to the moral law only through the protagonist and can experience the law only through the protagonist's experience of it. An example would be the dependence of Henry James' narrator on the limits of Maisie's knowledge in *What Maisie Knew*. Or the confrontation of the person as example may be that of one character by another within the tale, as, to stick with Henry James, Strether's confrontation of Chad in *The Ambassadors* generates all the story in that novel. Strether learns by way of what Chad learns, since he does not himself have Chad's transformative "learning experience."

One glimpses here a curious relation between the necessity of narrative in any discourse about ethics and the necessity of using analogies or figures of speech in place of an unavailable literal or conceptual language. Narrative, like analogy, is inserted into that blank place where the presumed purely conceptual language of philosophy fails or is missing. The relation of the character who is an example of the law to the law as such is figurative. The person is a synecdoche, part for whole and affirmed to be like the whole, as a sample of cloth is said to be like the whole cloth. This relation of person to law is a form of analogy or likeness, since the example is said to be like that of which it is an example. In being an analogy, the person who is an example of the law and thereby worthy of our respect is related to the law in a way analogous to the way fear and inclination are related to respect for the law. The exemplary person is not the law. He is in a certain sense not even like the law. How can a particular person be said to be like a universal law? But he is in another sense like the law. If we can never confront the law as such, we *can* confront the person who is an example of the law, just as fear and inclination are feelings we can understand and define and which we move into the place of respect which cannot be understood and defined in so many literal words. Confrontation with a person who is an example of the law stands in the place of, substitutes for, is a figure of, the law which is in no place we can reach and enter. The law is always somewhere else or at some other time, back there when the law was first imposed or off to the future when I may at last confront it directly, in unmediated vision. Within that space, between here and that unattainable there of the law as such, between now and the beginning or the end, narrative enters as the relation of the search for a perhaps impossible proximity to the law. If the authority of narrative, its coherence and force as a story, depends on that proximity to the law which would be defined by saying that the narration, like a person, is worthy of our respect because it is an example of the moral law as such, a clear manifestation of its productive force, then insofar as narrative takes place within the space of a perpetual deferral of direct confrontation with the law, it can be said that narrative is the narration of the impossibility of narrative in the sense of a coherent, logical, perspicuous story with beginning, middle, end, and paraphrasable meaning. The function of narrative, for those who have eyes to see and ears to hear with and understand, is to keep this out in the open.

Kant's obscure, evasive, and carefully concealed recognition both of the necessity of narrative in any account of the moral law as such and of the necessary failure of any narration to take the reader where he wants to be, face to face with the law, is expressed in the paragraphs in the main text of the *Grundlegung zur Metaphysik der Sitten* which follow just after the paragraph to which the footnote is appended. In the first of these following paragraphs the entanglement of narration and ethics is obliquely revealed in Kant's insertion, just at this place in his argument, of his celebrated formulation that I should act, if I wish to act ethically, at all times and places as if the private maxim according to which I choose to do or not to do were to be made the universal law for all mankind. How do I know I am acting ethically? I must ask myself what would happen if a law were made commanding everyone, everywhere at all times, to act also in just that way in such a situation. I must act in such a way (als so) that it is as if I were assuming that to be the case. In that "as if" a whole fictive narrative is implicit. Here are Kant's words, or rather the words of his translator, with some of Kant's own words inserted parenthetically:

"But what kind of law can that be, the conception of which must determine the will without reference to the expected result? Under this condition alone the will can be called absolutely good without qualification. Since I have robbed the will of all impulses which could come to it from obedience to any law [die ihm aus der Befolgung irgend eines Gesetzes entspringen könnten], nothing remains to serve as a principle of the will except universal conformity of its action to law as such. That is, I should never act in such a way that I could not also will that my maxim should be a universal law [d. i. ich soll niemals anders verfahren, als so, *daß ich auch wollen könne, meine Maxime solle ein allgemeines Gesetz werden:* A more literal translation would be: "That is, I should never act in any other way than in such a manner that I could also will that my maxim should be a universal law.'] Mere conformity to law as such (without assuming any particular law applicable to certain actions) serves as the principle of the will, and it must serve as such if duty is not to be a vain delusion and chimerical concept [ein leerer Wahn und chimärischer Begriff]. (E, 21; G, 28)

Kant's tone here is so reasonable, so blandly affirmative and apodictic, that what is extraordinary about his theory of ethics may slip by the reader. A truly moral act, he says, the act of a will absolutely good without qualification (ohne Einschränkung) must not only be performed without consideration of the expected result. It also must not be based on "obedience to any law" (aus der Befolgung irgend eines Gesetzes). Obedience to the law must not be based on obedience to any law. It is all very well to say that Kant means on the one hand any particular law, the law against adultery or the law against lying, for example, and on the other hand the "law as such," the fundamental principle of lawfulness, free of any particularity or delimitation. To say that only brings the paradox (if that is the word for it) more fully into the open in revealing the apparently uncrossable abyss between the law as such and any particular moral law which we might be able to use as a standard of judgment and obey or not obey. What kind of code of ethics or table of "Thou shalts" and "Thou shalt nots" is it which is wholly detached, apparently irrevocably detached, from any ascertainable connection to the principle of law as such on which it should be grounded? On the other hand, what can one say of a law as such, presumed foundation or *Grundlegung* of all morals, that is detached from all embodiment in any particular code of ethics and seems to give me no directions about how to act in a particular case, or at best directions which seem to be exceedingly evasive and indirect? In order to act morally I must act with complete indifference to any expected results of my actions, good, bad, or indifferent, for others or for myself, and I must act in abstraction from any impulse of obedience to any particular moral law. In order to act morally I must act immorally, or amorally, out of pure self-wrought universal conformity of my action to the law as such (die allgemeine Gesetzmäßigkeit der Handlungen). But how in the world am I going to make my actions conform to (in the sense of fit, be suitably measured by) a law which is without law, so purified of any identifiable content that it seems utterly useless as a standard of action in any practical sense? The law seems to impose on me a double interdict. On the one hand, it exists as an interdict against approaching it, confronting it directly, taking possession of it, giving it any specific content, for example in the verbal enunciation of the law as such. On the other hand, the law is an interdict against crossing over the gulf between the law as such and any particular maxim I might formulate on the basis of which I might decide how to act in a given case. If I am to act morally I must not act out of calculation of consequences, nor out of obedience to any particular law. I seem to be caught in an impossible double bind. Either way I have had it. And yet I must act. I must choose. Not to act is an act, not to choose a choice, and I want with all my heart to act morally, to be able to say that what I do I do out of absolute duty, do because I must do it. Unless I can find some way to ground my decision, my choice, my action on the law as such, duty will be no more than another name for doing what one likes, groundless and insubstantial, "a vain delusion and chimerical concept," a will-o'-the-wisp.

Kant's solution to this apparently insoluble knot in thinking is just the place where the necessity of narrative enters into his theory of ethics. We must, he says, perform a little experiment, enter in imagination into a little fiction, an "in such a way" or "als so." I must pretend that my maxim, that is the particular ethical rule by which this particular action is guided, were to be a universal legislation for all mankind. It is an act of imagination, like writing a novel. When I enter in imagination into the miniature novel I have created for myself, then I shall be able to tell in a moment whether or not my action is moral. Narrative as a fundamental activity of the human mind, the power to make fictions, to tell stories to oneself or to others, serves for Kant as the absolutely necessary bridge without which there would be no connection between the law as such and any particular ethical rule of behavior. Just as the blank place where respect is indefinable, can be given no predicate, is filled by the figurative analogy with fear and inclination, two things respect is not, and just as art or the work of art is defined in Kant's third critique, the *Critique of Judgment,* as the only possible bridge between epistemology, on the one hand, the work of pure reason, and ethics, the work of practical reason, on the other (which would otherwise be separated by the great gulf, *die grosse Kluft* between them),[4] so here within the theory of the practical reason itself another chasm opens up. This chasm too can only be bridged by a species of artwork, though one not openly defined as such by Kant. Across the gap between the law as such and the immediate work in the real world of the practical reason must be cast a little fictional narrative. This narrative must be on both sides of the gulf at once, or lead from the one to the other. It must be within the law as such, and it must at the same time give practical advice for the choices of the pure will in a particular case in the real work of history, society, and my immediate obligations to those around me. If the story I tell myself is a fictional narrative, it must be at the same time firmly implanted, like a bridge's abutments, on both sides of the chasm, in the law as such, which is no chimera, and in the real world where my choices and actions have real effects.

But the story I must tell myself is not just any anecdote involving the ethical choice which is in question for me. Such an imaginary anecdote would return me to the calculation of expected results or to the action out of fear or inclination which Kant has firmly rejected as offering no valid grounds for choice. The story I must tell myself is a miniature version of the inaugural act which creates a nation, a people, a community. I must act as though my private maxim were to be universal legislation for all mankind. In the fiction of this "in such a way" universal and particular, public and private, the law as such and a particular code of behavior, are bridged, and I become myself an example of the moral law, worthy of respect. The implied story in such an "als so" is the grand historical story of the divinely sanctioned law-giver or establisher of the social contract, Moses, Lycurgus, or the framers of the Declaration of Independence or of the Rights of Man. In every moral act I must behave as if I were like someone or a small group who make a definitive and revolutionary break in history, ending one era and starting another, as Moses came down from Sinai with the tablets of the law, handing down that law, or laying it down in an act that was radically inaugural, a new beginning for his people. Such an act creates the social order. It establishes the code of law which makes a people a community, not just a lawless conglomeration in which each man's hand is against his neighbor. This inaugural act, moreover, has an implicit teleology. It creates history. It is the prolepsis of a story not only with a beginning but with a middle and an end. Like all founding legislation or drawing up of a social contract it makes a promise: if you follow this law you will be happy and prosperous; if you do not, disaster will follow. My act is not ethical unless I act in such a way that what I do implies a miniature version of this initiating act of lawgiving, and has implicit within it a miniature version of a universal historical narrative. It is the story of a people who are paradigmatic for all mankind, a story moreover which goes from the first beginning of that people to its promised millennial end in a universal reign of justice and peace. Only if I act according to the fiction of this particular "in

such a way" can I be an example of the law and worthy of the respect of others.

In the two paragraphs just after the one which I have been
reading, Kant follows up his universal prescription (always to
act as if my maxim were to be legislation for all mankind) by giving
a little example of the making of a private act a universal example.
He makes up a little story or fiction, an "als so" of the "als so," so we
can see in imagination the sort of thing he means. His procedure
is not too different from the use of novels as what George Eliot
calls "experiments in life." We read novels to see in a safe area of
fiction or imagination what would happen if we lived our lives
according to a certain principle of moral choice. We take the novel
as potentially an example of the moral law as such and as the basis
of a legislation for all mankind. All mankind ought to act as Maisie
does in *What Maisie Knew* or as Strether does in *The Ambassadors*
or as Maggie does in *The Golden Bowl*. The exact terms of the
example Kant proposes are an example of a particular form of
philosophical genius about which there would be much to say. This
is a choice of examples in the course of an argument which are
not only not innocent (no example is innocent) but which in open
or covert ways pose a fundamental challenge to just the conceptual
formulations the examples are apparently meant to exemplify and
support. The example undermines that of which it is posed as an
example.

"Let the question, for example [zum Beispiel], be:"
proposes Kant, "May I, when in distress, make a promise [ein
Versprechen tun] with the intention not to keep it?" (E, 21; G, 29).
He then goes in to distinguish two ways of thinking about this.
On the one hand I may make calculations of a prudential sort about
whether lying in this way will get me out of my fix, whether I am
likely to get away with it, whether I shall get in even more trouble
later on when it is discovered that I have lied in this way, and so
on. Such calculations, for example that of the man who promises
the cannibals a better meal later on if they do not eat him now,
have nothing whatsoever of moral about them. Even if I decide to
make it my habitual maxim not to make a promise I do not intend

to keep because I may get in even more trouble later on, "such a maxim is based only on an apprehensive concern with consequences" (nur die besorglichen Folgen zum Grunde habe) (E, 22; G, 29). It is not moral because it is based on fear rather than on respect for the law. It is based on prudent calculation of results, not on duty. It is easy to see that there might indeed be cases in which it would be prudent to lie in this way. My real duty reveals itself when I ask myself whether I would be content that my maxim about making false promises should be the basis of a universal legislation. Here is Kant's formulation of what happens when I tell this little story to myself, create a private "in such a way" or fiction:

> The shortest but most infallible way to find the answer to the question as to whether a deceitful promise is consistent with duty is to ask myself: Would I be content that my maxim (of extricating myself from difficulty by a false promise) should hold as a universal law for myself as well as for others? And could I say to myself that everyone may make a false promise when he is in difficulty from which he cannot otherwise escape? I immediately see that I could will the lie but not a universal law to lie. For with such a law there would be no promises at all, inasmuch as it would be futile to make a pretense of my intention in regard to future actions to those who would not believe this pretense or—if they overhastily did so—who would pay me back in my own coin. Thus my maxim would necessarily destroy itself as soon as it was made a universal law. (E, 22–23; G, 29–30)

As I have said, the motif of making promises is already implicit in the formulation about acting as if my maxim were to be universal legislation for all mankind, so this little narrative of the man making a false promise is already latent in the law of which making false promises is given as merely one example among many. In fact the example is not random but essential. It is implicit as a fundamental aspect of the concept of which it is an exemplification. It is therefore not really an example but a bringing to the surface of the narrative implicit in the concept.

Making promises, moreover, is in two ways subversive of the apparent meaning of the concept of moral action. Making

promises, first, is not just any act. It is a specifically linguistic act.
It is, in addition, an example of that particular kind of linguistic
event called a performative. Making a promise, like betting, excusing,
and the like, is a way of doing things with words. The fact that
the example Kant chooses is linguistic opens the possibility that
the moral law is not just named in words but is brought into
existence in words. The fact that the example is not just any form
of language but a form which is performative doubles this possibility
with a further possibility inherent in all performatives, namely the
possibility that it will be impossible ever to confirm with certainty
whether the form of language in the performative makes happen
what it promises will happen. A performative makes something
happen, but, it may be, whether or not it makes happen what it
says will happen or intends will happen can never be known for
certain. In one direction, then, a promise is "undecidable" because
its authority is uncertain. It cannot be known whether it is based
on something outside itself or whether it creates its own autonomous
authority in the act of being made. In the other direction its teleology
is uncertain. The keeping of a promise is a matter of time or of
temporality, the matching of one time, the time of the promising,
with another time, the time of the keeping of the promise. That
second time may be indefinitely deferred or postponed. But these
are just the two things Kant wants the example to exemplify: on
the one hand the way a truly moral act is at once autonomous,
free, self-wrought, and at the same time based on respect for a
universal moral law which precedes it and gives it the law, so to
speak, and on the other hand the way such an action can be made
the basis of a universal legislation for all mankind, promising them
happiness, social stability, and prosperity.

The example Kant chooses is therefore not innocent. It
goes against the grain of the argument Kant seems to want above
all to secure. He wants to persuade his readers that respect for the
law is self-wrought but at the same time determined by a law which
precedes it and is external to it. This law exercises over me an
implacable necessity, a categorical imperative. I may discover this
irresistible coercion, for example, by trying to act contrary to it.

The example Kant gives, however, is of a special kind of performative language, the promise. A promise creates its own conditions of obedience in a temporalization requiring a comparison of before and after. Today I make a promise which later on I shall keep or not keep. The validity of the promise does not lie in itself but in its future fulfillment. It may be argued that this future fulfillment is never certainly confirmed, which is to say that it can never be confirmed that a promise has been kept, since something might always be done later on to invalidate my apparent fulfillment of my promise. A promise intrinsically demands an indefinite postponement of its fulfillment. For example, if I promise to be faithful to the woman I marry, it is always possible that after a lifetime of faithfulness I shall at the last minute betray her. In the same way, as I promise to show in a later book, my examples of novels by Eliot, Trollope, and James promise an ultimate bringing of the moral law into the open. This exposure, however, is always postponed, so that one can say the novels betray the promises they make. They impose on the reader the experience of a betrayal like that of being betrayed by his or her beloved.

This differential, deferential, or, as Jacques Derrida would say, "differantial," feature of the law, the way it both is divided within itself and at the same time defers, postpones, its validation, is the place where narrative and the law come together. Narrative can be defined as the indefinite postponement of that ultimate direct confrontation of the law which narrative is nevertheless instituted to make happen in an example worthy of respect. In the space between the promise and the perpetually deferred fulfillment of the promise the story takes place. The law itself, it would seem, is differentiated within itself, inaccessible because of that, and the story is divided against itself in response to that differentiation, out of respect for the division of the law within itself. Such a narrative leaves its readers at the end as dissatisfied as ever, still in expectation of the fulfillment of the promise which was the whole reason for being of the story. What the good reader confronts in the end is not the moral law brought into the open at last in a clear example, but the unreadability of the text. This unreadability is to be defined as the fact that the text commits again the error it denounces, namely, in this case, the error of claiming to be able to speak directly for the law and with the direct authority of the law. That I shall demonstrate that this is the case with certain exemplary novels is a promise I hereby make. Whether or not I succeed in keeping that promise I must leave it to my readers later on to decide. Meanwhile, in the space between that promise and its fulfillment, I can in this preliminary book discuss examples of that special kind of narrative text, the story of an author's reading of himself or herself.

In this case, here and now, as a conclusion to this section of my argument, I turn back to the little hypothetical story Kant proposes as an example reading, so to speak, his formulation about making my maxim the basis of a universal legislation. It might be remembered at this point that, as Paul de Man observes in his essay on Rousseau's *Social Contract,* the act of legislation involved in the establishment of a social contract, the initiating act establishing a society or a state, is an example of that form of performative called a promise. It therefore has just those ambiguities and fissures I have identified as intrinsic to a promise. The act of establishing a state is so subversive an act, it makes so clean a break with the past, that the lawgiver regularly and by a seemingly inevitable necessity claims divine or transcendent authority for the law he lays down, even though he has clearly demonstrated the nonexistence or unavailability of that authority in his first act of rebellion in order to justify his new beginning. In the other temporal direction the fulfillment of the promise in a happy society is always postponed yet a little further, with yet another five-year plan or yet another reaffirmation of the contractual law, however many years have passed since the inaugural legislation first established the state. As de Man says at the end of his essay on the *Social Contract,* in a brilliant and subversive alteration of Heidegger's formulation, *Die Sprache spricht:* "The reintroduction of the promise, despite the fact that its impossibility has been established (the pattern that identifies the *Social Contract* as a *textual* allegory), does not occur at the discretion of the writer. . . . The redoubtable efficacy of the text is due to the rhetorical model of which it is a version. This model is a fact of language over which Rousseau himself has no control. Just as any other reader, he is bound to misread his text as a promise of political change. The error is not within the reader; language itself disassociates the cognition from the act. *Die Sprache verspricht (sich);* to the extent that is necessarily misleading [sic], language just as necessarily conveys the promise of its own truth. This is also why textual allegories on this level of rhetorical complexity generate history."[5] Language promises, but what it promises is itself. This promise it can never keep. It is this fact of language, a necessity beyond the control of any user of language, which makes things happen as they do happen in the material world of history. History therefore is, as Kafka's priest puts it in my epigraph, necessary but not true.

In the case of Kant's little textual allegory in the paragraphs with their footnote I have been trying to read, Kant promises that an example involving promises will make clear the relation of the universal law to the particular case. The example, he assures us, will serve as the safe bridge between the one and the other. Instead of that, the example divides itself within itself between two possible but incompatible readings and so becomes unreadable. The bridge which was to vault over the abyss between universal and particular law opens another chasm within itself. In this case it is the impossibility of deciding whether the immorality of making a promise I do not intend to keep is really an example of a maxim founded on the law as such or whether it is only an example of the way civil order is a fact of language. In the latter case, society would be seen as depending altogether on conventions of language whereby words must go on meaning the same if men and women are to live together in society. An agreement to keep the rules of language the same would then be the foundation of civil order, not the law as such. One might see this as a version of utilitarianism. Who cares whether the state rests "on the basis of" anything, has any "ground" or *Grundlegung,* so long as its laws work and lead to the greatest happiness of the greatest number? In this version of utilitarianism, however, society would rest on the extremely

precarious ground of a linguistic contract. Such a contract is liable
to be broken at any moment. Indeed it necessarily breaks itself all
the time, if language has the features of necessary internal contradiction de Man says it has. If the possibility of making a lying
promise were made a universal law, says Kant, "there would be no
promises at all, inasmuch as it would be futile to make a pretense
of my intention in regard to future actions to those who would not
believe this pretense or—if they overhastily did so—who would pay
me back in my own coin. Thus my maxim would necessarily destroy
itself as soon as it was made a universal law." It is impossible to
tell whether this means society depends on a purely human and
linguistic contract, or whether it means that there is somewhere an
implacable transcendent law against making false promises. Moreover, Kant's formulation does not even give the reader any directions
for how one might go about distinguishing between those two
possibilities, even though everything hangs on being able to decide
which is the correct hypothesis.[6]

       Kant's example therefore does not exemplify that of
which it is meant to be an example. *Versprechen* as promise here
becomes a *Versprechen* in its secondary meaning of "slip of the
tongue." When that happens *versprechen* as "to promise" becomes
widersprechen, "to contradict," and the discourse as a whole becomes
a *Widersprechung,* a contradiction, something that contradicts itself.
There is always a latent contradiction in that German prefix *ver,*
which may be either an intensive or, conversely, a privative, a
negation. Kant says something other than what he means to say.
This something betrays a hidden flaw in his argument and makes
that argument a non sequitur or an anacoluthon, a failure in
following. The example of the man who makes a promise intending
not to keep it is like a bridge that does not meet in the middle,
but starts off from either bank and remains incomplete, with a gap
where the joining ought to be. What Kant promises to show is
that the law as such grounds a particular law against making lying
promises. What he actually shows by his little imaginary story is
that the social order depends on a precarious intralinguistic and
interpersonal agreement to go on meaning the same thing by words.

A lying promise is like a private language in that it is impossible
with either to count on the internal rules and conventions governing
language to remain stable or consistent. If, however, it is an intrinsic
feature of language, and especially of that kind of performative
called a promise, for example Kant's promise that his example will
conclusively demonstrate the categorical necessity of the law, that
it makes promises it cannot keep, so that the facts of language
exceed the intentions of its users, then that autodestruction Kant
describes ("Thus my maxim would necessarily destroy itself as soon
as it was made a universal law.") will occur whatever my intention.
It is an intrinsic feature of promises as a mode of language use
that they destroy themselves in this way.

    To put this more precisely, intending is another kind
of performative, like promising itself. Kant's example contains in
fact a double use of performative language. First I promise so and
so, to give the cannibals a better meal later if they do not eat me,
to be faithful to my wife. Then, or at the same time, I intend or
do not intend to keep the promise. The first performative is ratified
by second performative, as though the first were not enough in
itself. It is not enough to enunciate a promise. I must also enact
a second performative, the intention to keep the promise. The
problem is that an intention may be, and in this case clearly is,
enunciated only privately. I say to myself that I intend to keep the
promise that I have made, or I say to myself that I do not intend
to keep it. The intention not to keep it is what makes it a lying
promise. A private intention, however, is like a private language,
that is, it is vulnerable to the argument Wittgenstein makes against
its possibility. Like a private game, a private language has no
independent measure by which it is possible to be sure that its
rules remain the same from moment to moment. A private language
is therefore no language, or there is no such thing as a private
language. The same thing may be said of that special kind of
performative called a private intention. The unsettling or even ter-
rifying implication latent in Kant's example is therefore the possibility
that in the end it may not be possible to distinguish between a
promise made with the intention to keep it and one made with the

intention not to keep it. This is so because neither form of intention is open to objective measurement of its consistency and validity. Such enclosure cuts the promise off from its intention and makes it another example of that disjunction between necessity and truth which Joseph K., in my epigraph from Kafka, says is a "melancholy conclusion." It is more than simply melancholy. It is in fact an unmitigated disaster, since "it turns lying into a universal principle." Whether I intend to lie or do not intend to lie I lie in any case, by an intrinsic necessity of language.

The endpoint of my reading of my first example of the ethics of reading in action has led to the encounter with the unreadability of the example. On the one hand Kant asserts the rules whereby one can be certain to act ethically. He demonstrates the function of narrative as an essential part of that assertion, namely as the bridge between the law as such and any particular law applied in a specific familial, social, and historical situation. On the other hand, the story Kant tells, the story of the man who makes promises intending not to keep them, is undecidable in meaning. It therefore leaves the question open. The reader cannot decide whether the morality of promising is grounded in the law as such or whether it is an example of an ungrounded act which would define morality as a linguistic performative to be judged only by an internal temporal consistency which the example shows, as by a slip of the tongue, can never be attained. The unreadability of the text is to be defined as the text's inability to read itself, not as some failure on my part to read it. Having argued that a duty which is cut off from clear grounding in the law as such is no duty but a vain delusion and chimerical concept, Kant goes on in his example to show that it is never possible to be sure that duty is not a fiction in the bad sense of an ungrounded act of self-sustaining language, that is, precisely a vain delusion and chimerical concept, a kind of ghost generated by a sad linguistic necessity.

As Martin Heidegger argues in paragraph 31 of *Kant und das Problem der Metaphysik,* the paragraph just after the one in which he discusses Kant's theory of respect, it was Kant's "recoil" from recognizing what his thought was leading him toward, namely toward a concept of the founding power of the transcendental imagination, that marked the turning point in that thought. The unaided human imagination, transcendental or otherwise, came to seem to Kant a vain delusion and chimerical concept. He had at all costs, even the cost of suppressing his own most fundamental insight, to persuade himself that the human imagination is grounded in something beyond itself, namely in the law as such.

The reader of these paragraphs in Kant, with their appended footnote, is left, then, hovering in uncertainty, betrayed by the text. The text has not given him what it seemed to promise, a clear understanding of the ethics of reading. To appropriate Kant's own metaphor, I have been paid in counterfeit coin and have been forced to pay back bad treatment in its own coin, by a failure to find a certain ground for the ethics of reading in Kant's theory of ethics. I have been obliged by an inevitable necessity which may be the true ethics of reading (a strange truth in which lying becomes a universal principle), to pass this counterfeit coin on to my readers, just as those good citizens in Kant's little parable pay back the one who has made lying promises in his own coin.

In this fix the obvious move is to go to other passages where similar issues are exemplified and to try to read *them*. Only in this way can I find out whether what has happened to me when I have tried to read Kant is exemplary of the ethics of reading, paradigmatic, or whether it is an unlawful aberration, a kind of accident or *Versprechen,* an unfortunate slip of the tongue. I shall begin this further search in the next chapter with a passage about "ethicity" from Paul de Man, hardly a Kantian in the ordinary sense, as one example from "literary theory," and then go on in the following chapters to examples from novelists proper.

CHAPTER THREE

Reading Unreadability: de Man

Allegories are always ethical, the term ethical designating the struc-
tural interference of two distinct value systems. In this sense, ethics
has nothing to do with the will (thwarted or free) of a subject, nor
a fortiori, with a relationship between subjects. The ethical category
is imperative (i.e., a category rather than a value) to the extent that
it is linguistic and not subjective. Morality is a version of the same
language aporia that gave rise to such concepts as "man" or "love"
or "self," and not the cause or the consequence of such concepts.
The passage to an ethical tonality does not result from a transcendental
imperative but is the referential (and therefore unreliable) version of
a linguistic confusion. Ethics (or, one should say, ethicity) is a
discursive mode among others.

(Paul de Man)[1]

Every construction, every system—that is, every text—
has within itself the ignorance of its own exterior as the rupture of
its coherence which it cannot account for.

(Hans-Jost Frey)[2]

This chapter attempts to "read" the passage I have cited from
Allegories of Reading (in defiance of Paul de Man's assertion
that a critical text, as soon as it is taken as a text, is as "unreadable"

as any other text). What de Man means by "unreadable," something far different from widespread notions that it has to do with the "indeterminacy" of the meaning of the text, will be one of my concerns. My choice of the question of "ethics" in de Man is meant to further my investigation of what it might mean to speak of an "ethics of reading" through the reading of an example drawn from literary criticism or "theory," after the example from philosophy and before the properly "literary" ones from Trollope, Eliot, and James. My choice is also intended to confront frequent charges that de Man's work is "nihilistic," undermines the value of all humanistic study, reduces the work of interpretation to the free play of arbitrary inposition of meaning, finds in each text only what it went there to look for, and so on. What de Man actually says is so far from all this that it is a kind of puzzle to figure out how such ideas about his work have got around and pass current as valid intellectual coinage. Perhaps such ideas are just that, clichés passed from hand to hand by those who have never bothered to read de Man's work, no easy task, as I began by admitting.

"My" passage comes in the essay in *Allegories of Reading* entitled "Allegory *(Julie)*." This essay follows the one entitled "Self *(Pygmalion)*," and comes just before the one entitled "Allegory of Reading *(Profession de Foi)*." Other essays, in turn, come before and after each of those. My extract, in short, is abstracted from an intricate sequence of discursive and narrative argumentation in *Allegories of Reading* as a whole. The sequence of essays in that book is by no means arbitrary, haphazard, or merely chronological according to the order of writing, though exactly what story the book "as a whole" tells is another question. In any case, the act of abstraction I have performed in my initial citation is both necessary and at the same time illegitimate, unauthorized, as is always the case in such cases. The critic must make citations or refer to them, but cannot cite, for example, the whole of *Allegories of Reading*. Nevertheless, the citation cut off from its context takes on a different meaning, becomes a son with no father, defenselessly wandering the world, more likely to be vulnerable to my misreading.

Beyond that difficulty, presumably de Man's dictum that "a totally enlightened language, regardless of whether it conceives of itself as a consciousness or not, is unable to control the recurrence, in its readers as well as in itself, of the errors it exposes" (AR, 219) applies as much to the text of *Allegories of Reading* as to any other text, in a familiar recursive movement like that of the Cretan liar, disqualifying the affirmation in the act of making it. Moreover, what de Man says about the reader must apply also to me. I too must be unable to avoid repeating the errors I think I have seen and mastered by my reading of *Allegories of Reading*. That does not bode well for my fulfillment of the blithe promise to "read" a passage by de Man I made in my first sentence. I shall return later on to the question of just how this recurrence of error occurs in de Man and in me as a reader of de Man. Of course that final lucidity will in principle contain its own blind spot requiring a further elucidation and exposure of error, and so on, ad infinitum, with always a remainder of opacity. One should not underestimate, however, the productive illumination produced as one moves through these various stages of reading, as I shall now try to do.

By "the ethics of reading," the reader will remember, I mean that aspect of the act of reading in which there is a response to the text that is both necessitated, in the sense that it is a response to an irresistible demand, and free, in the sense that I must take responsibility for my response and for the further effects, "interpersonal," institutional, social, political, or historical, of my act of reading, for example as that act takes the form of teaching or of published commentary on a given text. What happens when I read *must* happen, but I must acknowledge it as *my* act of reading, though just what the "I" is or becomes in this transaction is another question. To say that there is a properly ethical dimension to the act of reading sounds odd, as I have said. It would seem that the act of reading as such must have little to do with ethics, even though the text read may make thematic statements which have ethical import, which is not at all the same thing. Reading itself would seem to be epistemological, cognitive, a matter of "getting the text right," respecting it in that sense, not a matter involving moral obligation.

Even less would Paul de Man's particular "theory" of reading seem likely to have an ethical dimension. Epistemological categories, categories of truth and falsehood, enlightenment and delusion, insight and blindness, seem to control the admirable rigor of his essays. The category of ethics or, as he says, "ethicity," does, however, somewhat surprisingly, appear at crucial moments in de Man's essays, for example in "my" passage. The category of ethicity is one version of that insistence on a necessary referential, pragmatic function of language which distinguishes de Man's work from certain forms of structuralism or semiotics. It also gives the lie to those who claim "deconstruction" asserts the "free play" of language in the void, abstracted from all practical, social, or political effect. Of de Man one can say what he himself says of Rousseau: "his radical critique of referential meaning never implied that the referential function of language could in any way be avoided, bracketed, or reduced to being just one contingent linguistic property among others, as is postulated, for example, in contemporary semiology which, like all post-Kantian formalisms, could not exist without this postulate" (AR, 207). Ethicity is for de Man associated with the categories of politics and history, though these three modes of what he calls "materiality" are not the same. My goal here is to account for the presence of the word "ethics" in de Man's vocabulary, and to present thereby a salient example within contemporary literary theory of an ethics of reading.

"Ethicity," like other forms of reference to the extralinguistic by way of the linguistic, occurs for de Man not at the beginning, as a basis for language, and not at the end, as a final triumphant return to reality validating language, but in the midst of an intricate sequence, the sequentiality of which is of course only a fiction, a convenience for thinking as a narrative what in fact always occurs in the tangle of an "all at once" mixing tropological, allegorical, referential, ethical, political, and historical dimensions. The passage I began by citing and propose in this chapter to try to "read" follows in *Allegories of Reading* on the page after one of de Man's most succinct formulations of his paradigmatic model for the narrative pattern into which all texts fall: "The paradigm for all texts consists of a figure (or a system of figures) and its deconstruction. But since this model cannot be closed off by a final reading, it engenders, in its turn, a supplementary figural superposition which narrates the unreadability of the prior narration. As distinguished from primary deconstructive narratives centered on figures and ultimately always on metaphor, we can call such narratives to the second (or the third) degree *allegories*" (AR, 205). This formulation is by no means immediately transparent in meaning. I have elsewhere attempted to read it in detail.[3] What is most important here is the fact that the ethical moment, for de Man, occurs toward the end of this intricate sequence, as primary evidence of a text's inability to read itself, to benefit from its own wisdom. First comes the assertion of an unjustified and aberrant metaphor, then the "deconstruction" of that metaphor, the revelation of its aberrancy, then the "allegory," that is, the expression in a veiled form of the impossibility of reading that revelation of aberrancy. One form that repetition of the first error takes is the mode of referentiality that de Man calls "ethicity."

The first feature of the ethical for de Man, then, is that it is an aspect not of the first narrative of metaphorical denomination, nor of the second narrative of the deconstruction of that aberrant act of denomination, but of the "third" narrative of the failure to read which de Man calls "allegory." Says de Man: "Allegories are always ethical." The ethical, or what de Man calls, somewhat barbarously, "ethicity," is not a primary category, but a secondary or in fact tertiary one. "Ethicity" is necessary and it is not derivative from anything but the laws of language that are all-determining or all-engendering for de Man, but the ethical does not come first. It intervenes, necessarily intervenes, but it occurs at a "later stage" in a sequence which begins with epistemological error, the error born of aberrant metaphorical naming. One must remember, however, that the sequential unfolding of "earlier" and "later" that makes all texts, in de Man's use of the term, "narratives" is the fictional temporalization of what in fact are simultaneous linguistic operations:

aberrant metaphorical naming, the deconstruction of that act of nomination, the allegory of the unreadability of those "first" two linguistic acts, and so on. Of that allegory of the impossibility of reading "ethicity" is a necessary dimension, since all allegories are ethical. In this sense ethicity is as first as any other linguistic act. It is unconditionally necessary.

But what does it mean to say that "allegories are always ethical"? It is clear that the main target of de Man's attack here is Kant's ethical theory. To put this another way, the passage about ethics simultaneously rejects Kant and bends Kantian language to another purpose. In order to make an open space for his own ethical theory, de Man has simultaneously to reject the Kantian theory and appropriate its language to his own uses: "The ethical category is imperative (i.e., a category rather than a value) to the extent that it is linguistic and not subjective." In order to argue that ethicity is the product of a purely linguistic necessity de Man has to reject the notion that it has to do with subjectivity, or with freedom as a feature of selfhood, or with interpersonal relations, or with a categorical imperative coming from some transcendental source, whether from subjectivity in the form of the transcendental imagination or from some extrahuman transcendence. "Ethics," says de Man, "has nothing to do with the will (thwarted or free) of a subject, nor *a fortiori,* with a relationship between subjects." And: "The passage to an ethical tonality does not result from a transcendental imperative."

Well, if ethics has nothing to do with any of the things it has traditionally been thought to be concerned with, with what then does it have to do? The answer is that ethical judgment and command is a necessary feature of human language. We cannot help making judgments of right and wrong, commanding others to act according to those judgments, condemning them for not doing so, responding ourselves to an ethical demand that will not be the less categorical and imperative for not coming from some transcendent extra-linguistic "law."

With the ground cleared of the chief alternative theories of ethics, especially the Kantian one, de Man can assert his own

purely linguistic theory. What, in his case, does this mean, and
how could an ethical judgment or command founded exclusively on
language have the authority necessary in ethics, the "I *must* do
this; I *cannot do otherwise,* and I *ought* not to do otherwise"? The
answer is that ethical judgment and command is a necessary part
of that narrative of the impossibility of reading that de Man calls
allegory. But what, exactly, does *this* mean? The failure to read,
the reader will remember, takes the form of a further, secondary
or tertiary, narrative superimposed on the first deconstructive narrative. This supplementary narrative shows indirectly, in the form
of a story, someone committing again the "same" linguistic error
that the deconstructive narrative has lucidly identified and denounced.
Only someone who can *read,* that is, who can interpret the allegory,
which seems to say one thing but in fact says something else, will
be able to see that what is really being narrated is the failure to
read. But that act of reading will no doubt commit another version
of the same error of the failure to read, and then again, in a
perpetual fugacity of final clarity. In "Reading (Proust)," an "earlier"
essay in *Allegories of Reading* that anticipates the procedures and
formulations of "Allegory *(Julie),*" de Man expressed this flight of
understanding by saying that "it is forever impossible to read
Reading" (AR, 77). Already in that essay he says that "any narrative
is primarily the allegory of its own reading," and that "the allegory
of reading narrates the impossibility of reading" (AR, 76, 77). *À la
recherche du temps perdu* is "read" as an example of the allegory
of the failure to read. It is an allegory in the sense that it says
one thing and means another. This "other," in de Man's theory of
allegory, is always "Reading," or rather the impossibility of reading
Reading. "Everything in [Proust's] novel," says de Man, "signifies
something other than what it represents, be it love, consciousness,
politics, art, sodomy, or gastronomy: it is always something else
that is intended. It can be shown that the most adequate term to
designate this 'something else' is Reading. But one must at the
same time 'understand' that this word bars access, once and forever,
to a meaning that yet can never cease to call out for its understanding" (AR, 77).

The category of the ethical or of "ethicity" intervenes, for de Man, just at this point where the act of reading bars access to an understanding of the act of reading. We can do it. We can read, but we cannot understand what it is we are doing. This means that what we do is always aberrant, since the only thing worth understanding is Reading itself, the ground and foundation of the whole of human life, for de Man. The making of ethical judgments and demands is one necessary feature of this failure to read.

Just how is this? The answer is that ethical judgments and demands are one major example of that committing again of the linguistic error already deconstructed that manifests the failure to read in the form of a secondary or tertiary narrative. In the "primary" deconstructive narrative, says de Man, the "polarities of truth and falsehood . . . move parallel with the text they generate. Far from interfering with each other, the value system and the narrative promote each other's elaboration" (AR, 206). The example given of this is the first part of *Julie,* in which the joy born of the lucid deconstruction of the error of deifying the one we love generates and sustains the narrative. "Hence," says de Man, "the relative ease of the narrative pattern . . . of the story of passion in the first part of *Julie* which is said to be 'like a live source that flows forever and that never runs dry' " (AR, 206). "In the allegory of unreadability," however, "the imperatives of truth and falsehood oppose the narrative syntax and manifest themselves at its expense. The concatenation of the categories of truth and falsehood with the values of right and wrong is disrupted, affecting the economy of the narration in decisive ways" (AR, 206). What this means (if I "understand" it) is that one of the primary ways that the failure to read manifests itself at the allegorical level is in the making of value judgments, the uttering of ethical commands and promises ("You should do so and so"; "You will be happy if you do so and so.") for which there is absolutely no foundation in knowledge, that is in the epistemological realm governed by the category of truth and falsehood. In fact the lucid understanding of the falsehood in metaphorical denomination gained at the primary deconstructive level "ought" to lead to a reading of the ensuing ethical judgments as false, even though according to the ethical value system they may be "right." That this cognitive "ought" is always obstructed is the basic presupposition of de Man's theory of the ethics of reading.

The formulation that "allegories are always ethical" is therefore completed by a crucial definitional phrase: "the term ethical designating the structural interference of two distinct value systems" (AR, 206). If the reader steps back for a moment from the context of de Man's intricate argumentation he or she will probably agree with me that this is an exceedingly odd definition of the term ethical: "the structural interference of two distinct value systems"! For de Man the categories of truth and falsehood can never be reconciled with the categories of right and wrong, and yet both are values, in the sense of making an unconditional demand for their preservation. Surely one should want to dwell within the truth, and surely one should want to do what is right, but according to de Man it is impossible to respond simultaneously to those two demands. A statement can be true but not right or right but not true, but not both true and right at once.

Why is this? The answer is given in the four sentences that complete the paragraph I have been trying to read: "The ethical category is imperative (i.e., a category rather than a value) to the extent that it is linguistic and not subjective. Morality is a version of the same language aporia that gave rise to such concepts as 'man' or 'love' or 'self,' and not the cause or the consequence of such concepts. The passage to an ethical tonality does not result from a transcendental imperative but is the referential (and therefore unreliable) version of a linguistic confusion. Ethics (or, one should say, ethicity) is a discursive mode among others" (AR, 206). For de Man, as for Kant, the fulfillment of an ethical demand must be necessary. It must be something I *have* to do, regardless of other competing demands. It is in this sense that it is a category rather than a value. A value is a matter of more or less, of differential comparisons according to some measuring yardstick. A categorical obligation is absolute and unconditional. We must do it, whatever the cost. In de Man's case, however, the necessity is linguistic rather than subjective or the effect of a transcendental law. It is a

necessity to be in error or at the least confused, as always happens
when I attempt to make language referential, and I *must* attempt
to make it referential. I cannot do otherwise. In the case of ethics
it is a necessity to make judgments, commands, promises about
right and wrong which have no verifiable basis in anything outside
language. It is in this sense that ethics (or ethicity) is a discursive
mode among others. That is, ethics is not just a form of language,
but a running or sequential mode of language, in short a story.
Ethics is a form of allegory, one form of those apparently referential
stories we tell to ourselves and to those around us. De Man's
assertion that morality is another version of the same language
aporia that generates such concepts as "man" or "love" or "self"
tells us what kind of a story ethics tells. The reference of course
is to his account of the rise of concepts in the chapter on Rousseau's
Second Discourse in *Allegories of Reading* and to his demonstration
of the way the particular concepts "man," "love," and "self"
deconstruct themselves in Rousseau in the chapters on the *Second
Discourse, Julie,* and *Pygmalion,* respectively. The reader of "Metaphor *(Second Discourse)*" will remember de Man's account of the
way the spontaneously aberrant metaphor "giant" is replaced by
the deliberately falsifying concept "man" as the basis of the making
equal of men and women that is necessary to the formation of
social order. De Man's reading culminates in a striking formulation:
"The concept ['man'] interprets the metaphor of numerical sameness
as if it were a statement of literal fact. Without this literalization,
there could be no society. The reader of Rousseau must remember
that this literalism is the deceitful misrepresentation of an original
blindness. Conceptual language, the foundation of civil society, is
also, it appears, a lie superimposed upon an error" (AR, 155).

      Ethicity too, according to de Man, it would follow, is
no more than another version of the same necessary form of lying.
It is storytelling in more than one sense. An ethical judgment,
command, or promise is like the concept "man" both in the sense
that it has no ground in truth and in the sense that it universalizes
without grounds, makes equal the always different moral situations
in which men and women find themselves. An ethical command

says, "Thou shalt not ever lie," or "Thou shalt not ever make promises intending not to keep them," or "Thou shalt not ever commit adultery." Or rather, an ethical judgment is a lie but not a lie. It is by no means true, but at the same time it cannot be measured as false by reference to any possible ascertainable true ethical judgment. To it would apply that "melancholy conclusion" (trübselige Meinung) Joseph K. reaches in his discussion with the priest of Kafka's parable, cited as my epigraph for this book: " 'No,' said the priest, 'it is not necessary to accept everything [said by the doorkeeper at the outer gate of the law] as true, one must only accept it as necessary.' 'A melancholy conclusion,' said K. 'It turns lying into a universal principle.' "

For de Man ethical obligations, demands, and judgments work in the same way as the court system in *The Trial* works, or as the social contract works in Rousseau's theory, that is, as one perpetually unverifiable referential dimension of an irresistible law, in de Man's case a law of language. Ethicity is a region of human life in which lying is necessarily made into a universal principle, in the sense that ethical judgments are necessary but never verifiably true. The failure to read or the impossibility of reading is a universal necessity, one moment of which is that potentially aberrant form of language called ethical judgment or prescription.

It is in this context that we must understand a remarkable series of sentences in de Man's Foreword to Carol Jacobs' *The Dissimulating Harmony:*

> Understanding is not a version of one single and universal Truth that would exist as an essence, a hypostasis. The truth of a text is a much more empirical and literal event. What makes a reading more or less true is simply the predictability, the necessity of its occurrence, regardless of the reader or of the author's wishes. "Es ereignet sich aber das Wahre" (not *die Wahrheit*) says Hölderlin, which can be freely translated, "What is true is what is bound to take place." And, in the case of the reading of a text, what takes place is a necessary understanding. What marks the truth of such an understanding is not some abstract universal but the fact that it has to occur regardless of other considerations. It depends, in other

words, on the rigor of the reading as argument. Reading is an argument (which is not necessarily the same as a polemic) because it has to go against the grain of what one would want to happen in the name of what has to happen; this is the same as saying that an understanding is an epistemological event prior to being an ethical or aesthetic value. This does not mean that there can be a true reading, but that no reading is conceivable in which the question of its truth or falsehood is not primarily involved.

It would therefore be naive to make a reading depend on considerations, ethical or aesthetic, that are in fact correlatives of the understanding the reading is able to achieve. Naive, because it is not a matter of choice to omit or to accentuate by paraphrase certain elements in a text at the expense of others. We don't have this choice, since the text imposes its own understanding and shapes the reader's evasions. The more one censors, the more one reveals what is being effaced. A paraphrase is always what we called an analytical reading, that is, it is always susceptible of being made to point out consistently what it was trying to conceal.[4]

This luminous passage is one of the most important formulations de Man made about the ethics of reading and its relation to the epistemological dimension of reading. The understanding of a text is prior to its affirmation as an ethical value, but both are necessary. Both are bound to take place, even though they take place against the grain of the reader's or the author's wishes. "Take place" is de Man's translation of Hölderlin's "ereignet sich," in the lines from the late hymn, "Mnemosyne," that he cites, wresting them from their context. It is a context, by the way, that is extremely enigmatic and that might take years of study and commentary to begin to "understand," even though, if de Man is right, the first reading of Hölderlin's poem would cause its understanding to take place as a kind of foreknowledge. A reading "takes place" as an event in the real world. *Ereignis* is the German word for event. Martin Heidegger has singled out this word in various places for commentary and analysis in relation, precisely, to that notion of *topos* or place. Each event takes place in a place which its occurrence as event makes into a place, as opposed to a vacant space with no meaning or coordinates. The same thing may be said of each act of reading. It takes place as an event in a certain spot and turns that spot in a certain sense into a sacred place, that is, into a place which is inaugural. Reading too turns empty space into a locus where something unique and unforeseen has occurred, has entered into the human world, and where it will have such effects as it will have. An act of reading, moreover, takes place, as something which is bound to happen as it does happen, to a certain person in a certain psychological, interpersonal, historical, political, and institutional situation, for example to a teacher or to a student in a certain university, or to a reader in a public library who happens to have taken the book down from the shelf.

Readings that "take place" in this way are "true" in the special sense of being true to an implacable law of language, that is, the law of the failure to read, not truth of correspondence to some transcendent and universal Truth with a capital T. Though de Man's formulation here is in terms of the necessary "truth" of each reading, and though what he says makes it sound as if reading is a game in which we cannot lose, since we are bound to get it right, however limited we are as readers or however much our presuppositions about what the text is going to mean may seem to foredoom us to get it wrong, the careful reader of de Man, the reader for example of the passage which has been my main focus, will know that what is bound to take place in each act of reading is another exemplification of the law of unreadability. The failure to read takes place inexorably within the text itself. The reader must reenact this failure in his or her own reading. Getting it right always means being forced to reenact once more the necessity of getting it wrong. Each reader must repeat the error the text denounces and then commits again. By a strange but entirely cogent reversal which disqualifies the binary opposition between true and false, what de Man calls "true" (not truth) here is the unavoidable exigency to be true to the obligation to lie, in the special sense de Man gives to lying. It is lying in the sense that one necessary moment in any act of reading is the referential turn which draws ethical conclusions, makes ethical judgments and prescriptions. These are unwarranted but they *must* follow the reading of the text. Both that understanding and the lie of unwarranted ethical affirmations are *bound* to take place, since both are inscribed within the text as its own failure to read itself. The reader in his act of reading must be true to that pattern.

The fact that the relation between ethical statements and the knowledge language gives is always potentially aberrant in no way means that ethical judgments do not work, do not sustain society, are not good in their effects. Ethical judgment, or "ethicity" in general, works in fact in the same precarious way as the social contract in de Man's description of it. Its working is always threatened by its own lack of ground. It is sustained only by the fact that a group of people can be got to act as if it had a ground, that is, as if there were absolute justice in rewarding people for certain actions, punishing them for others. "Finally," says de Man:

> the *contractual* pattern of civil government can only be understood against the background of this permanent threat. The social contract is by no means the expression of a transcendental law: it is a complex and purely defensive verbal strategy by means of which the literal world is given some of the consistency of fiction, an intricate set of feints and ruses by means of which the moment is temporarily delayed when fictional seductions will no longer be able to resist transformation into literal acts. The conceptual language of the social contract resembles the subtle interplay between figural and referential discourse in a novel. (AR, 159)

Presumably de Man means here that the application of one or another feature of the social contract, for example its codification of ethical judgments into civil law, to actual cases, will be necessarily unjust in the same way as the application of a methaphorically based concept, for example "man," to the unique case is always unjust. As soon as the metaphorical is applied to the literal, or the moral law applied to the unique individual, we get something like the arrest, prolonged trial, and ultimate execution of Joseph K. for a crime he is not aware of having committed against a law he cannot confront: "Someone must have been telling lies about Joseph K., for without having done anything wrong he was arrested one fine morning."[5] Or we get something like what happens to Michael Kohlhaas, in Kleist's story of that name.

What is most precarious about that form of the social contract which takes the form of a general agreement to act according to a given system of ethical judgment is that it has no ascertainable basis outside itself. It has no basis in the universal laws of subjectivity, nor in the "literal" social or material worlds, nor in some transcendent lawgiving power, though, as de Man observes, the creation of a social order is such a violent and unjustified act that lawgivers always claim, like Moses, divine sanction for their inaugural prescriptions. An ethical judgment is always a baseless positing, always unjust and unjustified, therefore always liable to be displaced by another momentarily stronger or more persuasive but equally baseless positing of a different code of ethics. And yet the imposition of a system of ethics is absolutely necessary. It is necessary in the double sense that it *has* to be made and that there can be no civil society without it.

The example de Man here gives of a shift from *pathos* to *ethos,* the shift from epistemological subtlety to ethical naiveté, is the way Rousseau tells his readers that reading *Julie* will be good for them, that the book contains practical advice for husbands and wives. "The question," says de Man, "is not the intrinsic merit or absurdity of these pieces of good advice but rather the fact that they *have to be* uttered, despite the structural discrepancy between their intellectual simplicity and the complexity of the considerations on which they are predicated" (AR, 207). *Why* do they *have to be* uttered? This, so it seems to me, is just what de Man, on his own terms, is forever barred from making intelligible. Just as, for Kant, the moral law as such is by definition forever inaccessible, though it manifests itself in the necessity, the categorical imperative, of particular moral judgments and acts, so for de Man the linguistic necessity that forces us all to make ethical judgments that have no epistemological basis, that in fact fly in the face of our epistemological insight, can in principle never be understood. We can never read Reading. This means that we can never understand why we cannot read our own epistemological wisdom clearly enough to avoid making ethical statements or telling ethical stories that are contradicted, undermined, and disqualified by that wisdom.

Kant's *Grundlegung zur Metaphysik der Sitten,* discussed in chapter 2, ends with the following cheerfully positive formulation: "And so we do not indeed comprehend the practical unconditional necessity of the moral imperative; yet we do comprehend its incomprehensibility, which is all that can be fairly demanded of a philosophy which in its principles strives to reach the limit of human reason" (Und so begreifen wir zwar nicht die praktische unbedingte Notwendigkeit des moralischen Imperativs, wir begreifen aber doch seine *Unbegreiflichkeit,* welches alles ist, was billigermaßen von einer Philosophie, die bis zur Grenze der menschlichen Vernunft in Prinzipien strebt, gefodert werden kann).[6] The difference between de Man and Kant (and it is quite a difference) is that Kant can have confidence in the ability of language and reason to formulate an understanding of a nonlinguistic impossibility, whereas in de Man's case it is a matter of encountering the limits of the possibility of understanding the laws of language with language.

As Hans-Jost Frey puts this in the sentence I have cited as an epigraph: "Every construction, every system—that is, every text—has within itself the ignorance of its own exterior as the rupture of its coherence which it cannot account for." Language cannot think itself or its own laws, just as a man cannot lift himself by his own bootstraps. Nor can language express what is outside language. It can neither know whether or not it has reached and expressed what is outside language, nor can it know whether that "outside" is a thought, or a thing, or a transcendent spirit, or some linguistic ground of language, or whether it is nothing at all, since for de Man, as for Rousseau, sensation, perception, and thought are not separable from language, cannot occur separate from language. They are permeated by language through and through, or they *are* language. This means that though language cannot help posit its referentiality, it can neither verify nor disqualify that referentiality, though any piece of language necessarily puts in question the validity of its referentiality.

In his reading of Rousseau's *Profession du Foi du Vicaire Savoyard* de Man once more states this basic presupposition of Rousseau's (and of his own) theory of language in its relation to human existence:

> To the extent that judgment is a structure of relationships capable of error, it is also language. As such, it is bound to consist of the very figural structures that can only be put in question by means of the language that produces them. What is then called "language" clearly has to extend well beyond what is empirically understood as articulated verbal utterance and subsumes, for instance, what is traditionally referred to as perception. . . . The term "language" thus includes that of perception or sensation, implying that understanding can no longer be modelled on or derived from the experience of the senses. . . . We can conclude that the vicar describes judgment as the power to set up potentially aberrant referential systems that deconstruct the referentiality of their own elaboration. This description warrants the equation of judgment with figural language, extensively conceived. (AR, 234–235)

"Aberrant" here has to be taken in a special sense, as is generally the case with de Man's use of the word. Referential statements, or statements taken referentially, are aberrant not in the sense of wandering away from some ascertainable norm, but in the sense of being a perpetual wandering from beginning to end. They are therefore, strictly speaking, only to be called "potentially aberrant," since we have no way to measure whether or not they are aberrant. All we can know is that they may be in error.

One of Kafka's aphorisms expresses exactly the human situation for de Man, that is, the predicament of being perpetually within language, spoken by it rather than being able to use it as a tool of power, and condemned by that situation to what de Man consistently calls "aberrancy." "There is a goal but no way," says Kafka; "what we call the way is only wavering."[7] Of the laws of language language cannot speak except in language that disqualifies itself as knowledge in the moment that it posits itself as language. Whenever we think we have pushed beyond the borders of language we find that the region we have reached magically reforms itself as still or already included within the borders of language. Though language contains within itself the evidence of its own limitation, the knowledge of that limitation can never be formulated in a way that is wholly reasonable or clear, since any formulation contains the limitation again. This limitation has the double definition of the failure, on the one hand, of language ever to be other than fragmentary, its failure ever to form a complete and completely coherent system, and, on the other hand, the failure of the "user" of language ever to know for sure whether or not it has validly referred to what is outside language. Among the various forms of that potentially, but never certainly, aberrant referentiality, are those ethical judgments and promises which *have to be made,* though their justice or injustice can never be known for sure, in spite of the fact that they do not jibe with the epistemologically based judgments of truth and falsehood language enables us to make. Even the conspicuous fact that no ethical system has yet brought the millenium of universal justice and peace among men is no proof of the inadequacy of any or all of them, since we can never be sure that the continued sufferings of men and women in society are not the result of a failure to act consistently and totally on the basis of the right one of those systems of ethical judgment. I would even dare to promise that the millenium would come if all men and women became good readers in de Man's sense, though that promise is exceedingly unlikely to have a chance to be tested in practice.

Since "Reading," for de Man, includes not just reading as such, certainly not just the act of reading works of literature, but sensation, perception, and therefore every human act whatsoever, in this case my apparently limited topic of the ethical dimension of reading would include the necessary but forever potentially aberrant referentiality of what he calls "ethicity" in human life generally. For de Man the ethical is one (necessary and necessarily potentially aberrant) act of language among others, taking language in the inclusive sense which he gives it in "Allegory of Reading *(Profession de foi)."* Kant's concluding formulation in the *Grundlegung* would therefore in de Man's case have to be reformulated in a way that measures the difference, the great gulf, between them. De Man might have said: "And so we do not indeed comprehend the practical unconditional necessity of the moral imperative; nor do we even comprehend its incomprehensibility, since the moral imperative itself, along with the human reason which strives to comprehend the incomprehensibility of its necessity, are both aspects of language, and it is impossible to use language as a tool with which to comprehend its own limitations."

It is impossible to get outside the limits of language by means of language. Everything we reach that seems outside language, for example sensation and perception, turns out to be more language. To live is to read, or rather to commit again and again the failure to read which is the human lot. We are hard at work trying to fulfill the impossible task of reading from the moment we are born until the moment we die. We struggle to read from the moment we wake in the morning until the moment we fall asleep at night, and what are our dreams but more lessons in the pain of the impossibility of reading, or rather in the pain of having no way whatsoever of knowing whether or not we may have in our discursive wanderings and aberrancies stumbled by accident on the right reading? Far from being "indeterminate" or "nihilistic," however, or a matter of wanton free play or arbitrary choice, each reading is, strictly speaking, ethical, in the sense that it *has* to take place, by an implacable necessity, as the response to a categorical demand, and in the sense that the reader *must* take responsibility for it and for its consequences in the personal, social, and political worlds. Reading is one act among others, part, as Henry James says writing itself is, of the conduct of life, however unpredictable and surprising each act of reading may be, since the reader can never know beforehand what it is in this particular case of reading that is bound to take place. Such is the rigor of Paul de Man's affirmation of an ethics of reading. It imposes on the reader the "impossible" task of reading unreadability, but that does not by any means mean that reading, even "good" reading, cannot take place and does not have a necessary ethical dimension.

CHAPTER FOUR

Reading Writing: Eliot

After the rigors of Paul de Man's intricate argumentation about the ethics of reading, the reader, it may be, turns with some expectation of relief to chapter 17 of George Eliot's *Adam Bede*, "In Which the Story Pauses a Little," just as, within the chapter, Eliot's narrator turns with relief from paintings of "cloud-borne angels, from prophets, sibyls, and heroic warriors" to those Dutch genre paintings "which lofty-minded people despise."[1] Surely, the reader thinks, Eliot believed in a straightforward realism in narration and surely that was associated with a confidence that readers could get straightforward moral lessons from her novels. For Eliot, a story is validated by its truth of correspondence to historical, social, and human reality, a human reality assumed to exist outside language. This goes along with a conviction that the function of such truth-telling is to teach us to be good, to love our neighbors, by offering examples of such goodness and of the disastrous consequences of its lack. Let us, however, look narrowly at the language of that famous chapter 17 and try to read what it says. It will be "needful," to use one of her words and one of her metaphors, to question it closely, as if it were in the witness box narrating its experience upon oath.

The theory of realism proposed in chapter 17 of *Adam Bede* depends on the notion that there can be a literal, nonfigurative, truthtelling language of narration. "So I am content," says the narrator,

> to tell my simple story, without trying to make things seem better than they were; dreading nothing indeed, but falsity, which, in spite of one's best efforts, there is reason to dread. Falsehood is easy, truth so difficult. . . . Examine your words well, and you will find that even when you have no motive to be false, it is a very hard thing to say the exact truth, even about your own immediate feelings— much harder than to say something fine about them which is *not* the exact truth.

What, exactly, is this language, the words with which the novelist can say the exact truth about inner feeling or outer facts, without a fraction more or less, like a board cut by Adam Bede to perfect length and fit?

The theory of the *function* of such language in the chapter is clear. It is a version of the definition of mimesis which goes back to Aristotle. This theory is one of the constants of occidental metaphysics. The theory is an economic one, in the broadest sense of that term. In Eliot's case it is an economic theory heavily tinged with the language of Protestant ethics. In Aristotle's *Poetics* the function of mimesis is knowledge. Imitation is natural to man, and it is natural for him to take pleasure in it. He takes pleasure in it because he learns from it. He learns from it the nature of the things or persons imitated, which without that detour through mimesis would not be visible and knowable.

In chapter 17 of *Adam Bede* the argument is not so much that I should know my neighbor as that I should love him or her:

> These fellow-mortals, every one, must be accepted as they are: you can neither straighten their noses, nor brighten their wit, nor rectify their dispositions; and it is these people—amongst whom your life is passed—that it is *needful* you should tolerate, pity and love: it is

these more or less ugly, stupid, inconsistent people, whose movements of goodness you should be able to admire—(my italics)

It is more *needful* that I should have a fibre of sympathy connecting me with that vulgar citizen who weighs out my sugar in a vilely-assorted cravat and waistcoat, than with the handsomest rascal in red scarf and green feathers;—more *needful* that my heart should swell with loving admiration at some trait of gentle goodness in the faulty people who sit at the same hearth with me. (my italics)

The argument here, like Aristotle's, depends on the notion that, paradoxically, things, in this case one's neighbors, cannot be seen as they are, therefore cannot be loved and admired, in themselves. It is necessary that they make a detour through the mirroring of art in order to become visible and hence lovable. A parallel argument is made by Fra Lippo Lippi in his defense of a "realistic" art in Robert Browning's poem:

> God's works—paint any one, and count it crime
> To let a truth slip. Don't object, "His works
> Are here already; nature is complete:
> Suppose you reproduce her—(which you can't)
> There's no advantage! you must beat her, then."
> For don't you mark? we're made so that we love
> First when we see them painted, things we have passed
> Perhaps a hundred times nor cared to see;
> And so they are better, painted—better to us,
> Which is the same thing. Art was given for that;
> God uses us to help each other so,
> Lending our minds out . . .[2]

In Eliot's case the argument is that it is "needful," we have an "obligation," not only to reflect things accurately in the mirrors of our minds but to return that reflection with "interest," so to speak, that is, in a represented form. The reflection must be turned into a genre painting or into a realistic novel. This must be done in such a way that what is reflected will be seen, understood, and loved. The obligation is economic, legal, and ethical, all at once. Eliot's narrator, at the end of the chapter, says: "I herewith discharge my conscience." This is the fulfillment of a categorical imperative, the one thing needful. At the same time it is the fulfillment of a contract, as when one has borrowed money from the bank and must pay it back with interest, "discharge" the debt. At the same time, finally, it is the fulfillment of a legal obligation, as when one must tell the truth under oath in the witness box.

All three of these superimposed circuits of detour and return are guaranteed by their relation to a religious obligation. I must, in conscience, love God first and then love my neighbor as myself. The truthtelling of the witness is based on an oath sworn "before God," or "by God." The painter or novelist, in his return with interest of what his mind has reflected, imitates God in that productivity whereby all the creation emanated from God only to be returned to him with a plus-value of that chorus of praise all nature raises in speaking back the name of God to God. This is stated in concentrated form in the simultaneously indicative, imperative, and performative last line of Gerard Manley Hopkins' "Pied Beauty": "He fathers forth whose beauty is past praise,/Praise him." The syntax of this in the full grammar of the poem makes it mean at once: "All created things do praise him"; "Let all things praise him"; and "I here, in the poem, perform the act of praising him."

All three forms of the human circuit of detour and return, the economic, the ethical, and the legal, each grounded implicitly in the divine circuit of creation, and each functioning as a figure for the act of realistic representation, come together in Eliot's initial profession of obligation:

> But it happens, on the contrary, that my strongest effort is to avoid any such arbitrary picture, and to give a faithful account of men and things as they have mirrored themselves in my mind. The mirror is doubtless defective; the outlines will sometimes be disturbed, the reflection faint or confused; but I feel as much bound to tell you as precisely as I can what that reflection is, as if I were in the witness-box narrating my experience on oath.

The reflection here is double. This is true of the Victorian theory of realism generally, that system of intertwined figures and concepts about art or literature which governs in one way or another all Victorian discourse on that topic. Examples would include the abundant writings of Ruskin or, at the other end of a scale of complexity, the multitude of reviews of novels in Victorian periodicals. The diverse versions of this theory tend to be simultaneously subjective and objective in their notions about truth. They move uneasily back and forth between one and the other. The value of a novel, for Eliot, as for her contemporaries generally, lies in its truth of correspondence to things as they are, objectively. On the other hand, what is represented in the words of the novel is not the objective things as they are but those things as they have already been reflected in the mirroring mind of the novelist. That mirror, as Eliot here explicitly affirms and as her contemporaries agreed, always distorts. Subjectivity is like a mirror in a funhouse, concave, convex, or wavy, so that, as she says in a passage in *Middlemarch,* "I am not sure that the greatest man of his age, if ever that solitary superlative existed, could escape these unfavorable reflections of himself in various small mirrors; and even Milton, looking for his portrait in a spoon, must submit to have the facial angle of a bumpkin."[3] Even so, the novelist must represent as accurately as possible the reflection he finds in the defective mirror of his mind. The truth of correspondence in realism is not to objective things, or only indirectly to objective things. It is rather to things as they have already made a detour into necessarily distorted subjective reflections. Eliot's obligation is, as she says, "to give a faithful account of men and things as they have mirrored themselves in my mind."

From things to mental images to verbal account—the words on the page in a realistic novel are the product of a double translation. Their function is performative, not merely descriptive or cognitive. The obligation fulfilled in "the faithful representing of commonplace things" is to generate the right feelings in the reader or beholder of such representations. These feelings bring the people who feel them to do the right thing, for "it isn't notions set people doing the right thing—it's feelings." The double mirroring of a realistic art makes something happen. It makes the right things happen by making people do the right thing. Commonplace things as they are must be returned back into those things as they are, after their double excursis, first into the mirroring mind, and then into the words which give a faithful account of that mind. They must be reintroduced into the culture which produced the art and which that art represents. They must be returned with the plus value of a power to generate good feelings and therefore good actions. Only then is the "account" fully made and closed, the obligation fulfilled, the note discharged, the mortgage on the house of fiction paid off.

In the context of this economic-ethical-religious-affective-performative theory of realism George Eliot mounts his attack on idealizing art, the art of irrealism. (I say "his" to remind the reader that the putative speaker in this chapter is not Mary Ann Evans, the author of *Adam Bede,* but a fictive personage, "George Eliot," who narrates the story and who is given a male gender.) Eliot's attack on irrealism runs as a crossways woof through all the fabric of chapter 17, countering the positive argument. At first sight the attack on ideal beauty and goodness seems entirely reasonable. People are not like that, at least not those near home, and there can be no use, no obligation, nothing "needful," in representing them as they are not. Much more is at stake here, however, than may at first appear.

What George Eliot explicitly rejects in the counterwoven argument of the chapter is that theological underpinning which is implicit in the economic theory of realism I have traced out. Though it is not a question here of direct influence, the best shorthand description of what Eliot rejects would give it the proper name Immanuel Kant. It was by no means necessary to know Kant's works in order to be a Kantian or an anti-Kantian in the nineteenth century, nor is it so in our own day. Kant in the *Critique of Judgment* codified a set of notions about art which is one of the constants of the Western tradition. The genius, according to Kant, imitates nature not by copying it, but by duplicating its manner of production. As God spoke nature into existence by means of the divine word and by means of his Son, the Word, so the genius, by virtue of a power given him by nature, speaks into existence a heterocosm which adds something hitherto unheard-of to nature. It adds the plus value of a new beauty which is beyond price. This new beauty is beyond measure by any slavish standards of mirroring correspondence to things as they are. The novel beauty the genius creates is grounded in the analogy between his *logos* and the divine *logos*. This analogy is based in nature or goes by way of nature, though only because nature is the word of God, a voice made into substantial things. Analogy, as the word suggests, is always a similarity in voices or in words.[4]

This Kantism George Eliot rejects. He rejects it by removing its ground in the analogy between God's way of producing nature and the way the genius produces his works. Without this analogy the works of "genius" are simply unreal. They are a detour into the fictive from which there is no return to the real world of ugly, stupid, inconsistent neighbors. Therefore such works of art are of no use. They fulfill no obligation. They are the reverse of "needful."

George Eliot's way of expressing this is in several ways odd. It is odd for one thing in its effacement of the problem of language by a shift from language to another of the arts, painting. This sideways displacement occurs regularly throughout the chapter, for example in the famous appeal to Dutch genre painting as a model for truthtelling in literature. One effect of this is to make the reader forget the problem of the medium in literary realism. The implication is that the language of realism is a proper language functioning like a photograph or a scientific drawing. It goes by way of a one-to-one correspondence between the word and the thing.

The fact that language is the medium of realism and the fact that there are specific problems associated with the medium are intermittently confronted in the chapter. An example of one such problem which George Eliot at least implicitly recognizes is the temporality of narration. "An account of men and things as

they have mirrored themselves in my mind" is not a static spatial
picture but a running narrative going from word to word, according
to another meaning of "account" alongside the economic and ethical
ones. An "account" is a telling over, an enumeration one by one
of a series of items which are then added up to make a sum. In
another place, in a passage cited above, George Eliot reminds the
reader of the difficulty of finding the right word even for what is
closest at hand and most intimate, one's own emotions; "it is a
very hard thing to say the exact truth even about your own immediate
feelings." The shift from language to painting or drawing invites
the reader to forget all those problems which are specific to language.
It invites him to think of narration in language as like making an
exact atemporal drawing of something physically there before the
artist's eyes, a lion or a jug:

> So I am content to tell my simple story, without trying
> to make things seem better than they were; dreading nothing, indeed,
> but falsity, which, in spite of one's best efforts, there is reason to
> dread. Falsehood is so easy, truth so difficult. The pencil is conscious
> of a delightful facility in drawing a griffin—the longer the claws,
> and the larger the wings, the better; but that marvellous facility
> which we mistook for genius is apt to forsake us when we want to
> draw a real unexaggerated lion.

"The pencil is conscious"—it is an odd phrase. It seems
as though the phallic-shaped instrument of writing must have its
own impulse toward falsehood. The impulse toward falsehood is
given an implicit male gender, the gender of the narrator himself,
whereas the faithful representing of commonplace things is perhaps
therefore implicitly female. This may seem an implausibly large issue
to pin on an innocent metonymy assigning consciousness to the
means of writing rather than to the writer, but readers of *Middlemarch* or of Eliot's work as a whole will know that a contrast
between male and female imaginations is a major feature of her
work. Her work turns on a dismantling of the "phallogocentric"
male system of metaphysics and its replacement by what, remem-
bering one of the key metaphors of *Middlemarch,* one might call

Ariadne's performative "yes" to life. This speech act is dramatized in Dorothea's marriage to Will Ladislaw at the end of *Middlemarch*. I shall try elsewhere to demonstrate in detail how that works.

In chapter 17 of *Adam Bede*, to return to that, the facility of the conscious pencil which produces griffins is mistaken by the mind of the one holding the pencil for genius. It is taken in error as a God-given gift for generating works of art not copied from nature but nevertheless valid. In fact the conscious pencil produces nullities, empty fictions. This facility in falsehood is defined sardonically elsewhere in the chapter as "the gift of that lofty order of minds who pant after the ideal." The conscious pencil of the false genius produces by its lofty elevation those embodiments of religious, mythological, and heroic ideas which are so resolutely rejected throughout the chapter. They are rejected as "falsehoods" or at best as validated only in a Feuerbachian way as projections of purely human values. All those paintings of the Madonna, for example, are for George Eliot, as for Ludwig Feuerbach, to be venerated not because Mary was the Mother of God but because a Madonna in art embodies the ideal of human motherhood. It is as if George Eliot were prepared to hurry with averted face through all the rooms in the Louvre marked "Renaissance Painting, Italy," in order to get to the room of Dutch genre paintings with all the relief of a man escaping the temptations of a false ideal in order to confront once more the real:

> I turn, without shrinking, from cloud-borne angels, from prophets, sibyls, and heroic warriors, to an old woman bending over her flowerpot. . . .

> Paint us an angel, if you can, with a floating violet robe, and a face paled by the celestial light; paint us yet oftener a Madonna, turning her mild face upward and opening her arms to welcome the divine glory; but do not impose on us any aesthetic rules which shall banish from the region of Art those old women scraping carrots with their work-worn hands, those heavy clowns taking holiday in a dingy pothouse, those rounded backs and stupid weather-beaten faces that have bent over the spade. . . .

There are few prophets in the world; few sublimely beautiful women; few heroes. I can't afford to give all my love and reverence to such rarities: I want a great deal of those feelings for my everyday fellowmen, especially for the few in the foreground of the great multitude, whose faces I know, whose hands I touch, for whom I have to make way with kindly courtesy.

Rejecting an aesthetic of the sublime, the beautiful, the ideal, the rare, the distant, George Eliot affirms with great persuasive power a counter-aesthetic of the ugly, the stupid, the real, the frequent, the statistically likely, the near. It is the griffin replaced by the lion or, better, by the house cat. Once again the economic metaphor is essential. I have only so much love and reverence banked in my account of emotional savings, and I "can't afford" to squander it on ideal rarities, if indeed they exist at all. All my emotion is needed for those who are near at hand, those "more or less ugly, stupid, inconsistent people," my neighbors.

All this seems clear enough. It is consistent in its rejection not so much of the Kantian sublime as of a Kantism deprived of the analogy between the artist's voice and his power of production on the one hand, and the divine *logos,* with its performative power to make all by fiat, on the other.

Nevertheless, a question still remains. What exactly is the mode of language by which the novelist produces in literature something analogous to the adherence to the real of Dutch genre paintings? It would seem that the answer to this question would be easy to give. Surely the realistic novelist works primarily with referential, nonfigurative language, language validated by its truth of correspondence to things as they are. This is the sort of language that calls a spade a spade or an old woman scraping carrots an old woman scraping carrots.

As a matter of fact, the theory of language developed elsewhere in *Adam Bede* is considerably more problematic than this notion of referential literalism. This theory, dramatized in the way the characters live out, in the flesh, so to speak, problems of language, plays ironically against the notion of referential language affirmed in chapter 17 for the narrator's truthtelling. Though there is not space here for a demonstration of the way the action itself of *Adam Bede* dramatizes the age-old story of the disasters that follow taking figures of speech literally, it is needful for my reading of George Eliot's reading of himself to show that in fact the theory of language in chapter 17 is not so simple either. The question of the language of realism is the missing link in the chain of George Eliot's argument. This link can be reconstructed from the implications of the figures and negations he uses to tell the reader what that language is like and what it is not like. This process might be compared to the archeologist's reconstruction of the missing limb of an ancient statue or to the paleontologist's making of a complete skeleton from a few fossil bones. In this case too a rather unexpected animal emerges when the pieces are put together.

The question, the reader will remember, is what language will not only render a true account of things and men as they have mirrored themselves in the narrator's mind but also render that account in such a way as to add the interest of the one thing needful. The one thing needful is the creation of a fiber of sympathy tying the reader in love and reverence to his ugly, stupid, inconsistent neighbors. The narrator tells the reader that such language will be like genre paintings and unlike religious, mythological, or historical painting. Nothing is said about how one imitates in words the methods of those "Dutch paintings, which lofty-minded people despise." Exactly what linguistic procedures are involved?

The reader is told, at least implicitly, first by the narrator and then by Adam Bede himself in a long speech cited verbatim by the narrator from a conversation he had with Adam "in his old age," that the proper language of storytelling will be like the sermons of Mr. Irwine and unlike the sermons of Mr. Ryde. This is an odd moment in the novel. The narrator elsewhere in the text has been anonymous, invisible, omniscient, and omnipresent, able to move freely and instantaneously in time and space, able to see without being seen, able to enter into the minds and hearts of the characters at will. In this chapter the narrator narrows down to a single "real" person, dependent on individual reports for his information. This is

especially apparent in his description of his encounter with the old
Adam Bede. It is as if a cut-out photographed figure were inserted
by collage into a Dutch painting. About this more must be said
later. Now the question is the following: if the implicit comparison
with two kinds of preaching gives a model for storytelling which
is linguistic rather than graphic, what is the difference between
Irwine's sermons and Ryde's? Again the reader is told little except
negatively. Irwine, says Adam, "was [not] much of a preacher."
"[H]e preached short moral sermons, and that was all." Ryde, on
the other hand, preached sermons full of "notions" and "doctrines,"
but these forms of language were ineffective in making his parish-
ioners do the right thing and love their neighbors:

> "But," said Adam, "I've seen pretty clear ever since I was a young
> un, as religion's something else besides notions. It isn't notions sets
> people doing the right thing—it's feelings. . . . Mr. Ryde was a deal
> thought on at a distance, I believe, and he wrote books; but as for
> math'matics and the natur o' things, he was as ignorant as a woman.
> [Note, by the way, the irony of the last phrase, when one thinks of
> it as written not by "George Eliot" but by Mary Ann Evans, daughter
> of Robert Evans, the "original" of Adam.] He was very knowing
> about doctrines, and used to call 'em the bulwarks of the Reformation;
> but I've always mistrusted that sort o' learning as leaves folks foolish
> and unreasonable about business."

This seems to offer a clue to the proper language of
storytelling in a double displacement, first to the question of the
effective language of preaching and then from that to an apparent
analogy between language causing "feelings" or "resolutions" and
the language of mathematics, business, and "the natur o' things."
This shift goes by way of a bifurcation between notions and doctrines,
on the one hand, and some kind of language that will bring about
"resolutions," on the other. A measuring, hardheaded, literally
naming, referential language, dramatized in the novel in Adam's
profession of carpentry, seems to give the reader a model for the
proper language of narration. But no, somewhat surprisingly, both
the language of mathematics and the language of literal naming

are dismissed as of no account, as ineffective, as unable to generate feelings and the good actions that follow from them:

> It's the same with the notions in religion as it is with math'matics,—a man may be able to work problems straight off in's head as he sits by the fire and smokes his pipe; but if he has to make a machine or a building, he must have a will and a resolution, and love something else better than his own ease.
>
> But I've seen pretty clear every since I was a young un as religion's something else besides doctrines and notions. I look at it as if the doctrines was like finding names for your feelings, so as you can talk of 'em when you've never known 'em, just as a man may talk o' tools when he knows their names, though he's never so much as seen 'em, still less handled 'em.

If it is not the language of mathematics and if it is not the language of literal naming, then what is it? It must be some form of language which corresponds not to doctrines in religion, nor to the abstract calculations of mathematics, nor to the naming of tools but to doing something with those tools, to the performance of an action. Realistic fiction must make something happen in the pragmatic world of things and people. It must make the correct things happen. The search for the proper language of storytelling has eliminated one by one all the obvious candidates. The search has narrowed itself down into a corner where only one answer is possible. Realistic narration must depend, as this chapter of *Adam Bede* conspicuously does, on figurative language. Even more narrowly, it can be said to depend on a special form of figurative language: catachresis, the use of terms borrowed from another realm to name what has no literal language of its own. Only such language can perform into existence feelings, a will, a resolution. The operation of such catachreses is itself necessarily described in figure in the chapter, as like this or as like that, since it cannot be literally described in itself.

Such a language will make a break in the remorseless chain of cause and effect which ordinarily operates, for Eliot, both in the physical or social worlds and in the internal world of the self. Only such a break, a fissure dividing before and after, can effect a redirection of the power of feeling in the self. This produces a consequent redirection of the power of doing in the outer world of the neighbors of that self. The renaming of things by the figure called catachresis is genuinely performative. It brings something altogether new into the world, something not explicable by its causes. Even though, like all performatives, it must use words already there in the language, it redirects those words to unheard-of meanings. It makes something happen in the "real world" which would not otherwise have happened. This happening has no "basis" other than the fictive, figurative, reevaluation performed by the catachresis renaming one's ugly, stupid, inconsistent neighbors as lovable. George Eliot's language for this, or rather the language he borrows from Adam Bede, is borrowed from scripture, which borrows it from the natural world, in a multiple displacement, each realm of language supplementing a lack in the one of which it comes in aid. Just as the language of realism is catachresis, so it can only be spoken of as like this or as like that, as like religious experience, or as like violent changes in nature, which in turn are like religious experience. Realism is catachresis, and it can be named only in catachresis:

> "I know [says Adam] there's a deal in a man's inward life as you can't measure by the square, and say, 'Do this and that'll follow,' and, 'Do that and this'll follow.' There's things go on in the soul, and times when feelings come into you like a rushing mighty wind, as the Scripture says, and part your life in two a'most, so as you look back on yourself as if you was somebody else."

> "If we've got a resolution to do right, He gave it us, I reckon, first or last; but I see plain enough we shall never do it without a resolution, and that's enough for me."

In the context of what Eliot says elsewhere in this chapter about the fictive status of religious ideals, angels, Madonnas, and so on, the word "He" here, naming God as the base of sudden discontinuous changes in human feelings and actions, is another catachresis, perhaps the most extravagant of all. It gives the name

of the personified deity to what are in fact, according to Eliot and
according to her master-source, Ludwig Feuerbach, only human
feelings. To Adam it seems that God gives feelings which give the
proper resolutions. Eliot and the reader see plain enough that God
is a name for human feelings. They see that it is such performative
catachreses (for example religious language naming God as the
source of the rushing mighty wind in the soul) which function as
that force of change parting a man's life in two almost.

     Even though chapter 17 is strongly committed, in its
overt affirmations, to realism as exact reproduction, the covert
argument is for a use of figurative language. Such language does
not say directly what it means. The language of realistic fiction is
not based solidly on any extra-linguistic entities. It transforms such
entities into something other than themselves, as your ugly, stupid,
neighbor is made lovable when he or she has passed through the
circuit of representation in a "realistic" novel.

     One example of figurative language stares the reader in
the face in this chapter, so close at hand and so pervasive as to
be almost invisible. In this it is like the big name written all across
a map, and therefore undetectable, in Dupin's figure for the invis-
ibility of the obvious in Poe's "The Purloined Letter." In chapter
17 of *Adam Bede,* as in the novel as a whole, the example of this
is the voice of the fictitious narrator concocted by Mary Ann Evans.
This narrator speaks as a male "I." He speaks as if all these things
had really happened in history just as they are told. He bases his
defense of realism on the purported conversation of another fictitious
character, Adam Bede, and on Adam's analysis of religious experience. This kind of experience is shown elsewhere in the novel to
be a response to the "ideal" in the sense of the unreal. Religious
experience is a human projection, a fiction. The response of the
reader who knows the "source" of Adam in Mary Ann Evans' own
life is an uneasy oscillation. This is Mary Ann Evans reporting
accurately the speech and opinions of her father, thereby giving a
faithful account of men and things as they have mirrored themselves
in her mind. No, it is Mary Ann Evans pretending to be a male
narrator reporting the speech of another invented character, "based"

perhaps on her father, but transposed into the realm of fiction where it can function as a performative force. The transposition of the author to the narrator, her father to Adam, corresponds, on the larger scale of the creation of character, to that smaller scale creation of figures of speech whereby a literal word is carried over not to substitute for another literal word but to name something that has no name other than a figurative one. Such nomination does not so much name something that already exists as make something happen, in the "real" world, that would not otherwise have happened.

Like all performatives, this one is fundamentally ambiguous. Its "undecidability" is to be defined by the fact that it is impossible to know whether anything really happens as a result of its force, or whether it only happens fictively, so does not happen at all. Can one hold in fact to the distinction between a real event and a fictive one? Does something really happen when a marriage is performed, a ship christened, or does it only happen in imagination? This is precisely the issue in Eliot's Feuerbachian treatment of religious experience and religious practices. Even if it can be decided that performatives do make something happen, it can never be decided exactly what that something is and whether that something is good or bad. All performatives are unpredictable and unmeasurable. A performative can never be controlled, defined, or have a decisive line put around its effects. The link between knowledge and power goes by way of language, and that link is both a barrier and a break, a gulf. Language used performatively makes something happen all right, but the link between knowing and doing can never be predicted exactly or understood perspicuously after the fact.

The peculiar final paragraph of chapter 17 of *Adam Bede* uneasily recognizes this. In the attempt to discriminate his own good performative evaluations from the other bad ones, George Eliot inadvertently reveals the structural kinship of all three. He is like a man who confesses to a criminal act by compulsively making a point of denying that he has committed it. In this final paragraph something odd about the initial idea of a contractual debt almost comes to the surface as George Eliot, as he says, "discharge[s] [his] conscience." He pays this debt by confessing that he has had "enthusiastic movements of admiration" for "commonplace," "vulgar" people, people "who spoke the worst English." At the beginning of the chapter he affirms, as I have shown, that the realistic novelist has an obligation to return what has been given to him in social experience by making an exact copy that will pay the debt with interest. This interest is an added power to generate enthusiastic movements of admiration for the ugly and the commonplace. The word "enthusiastic" in its context rings with the irony of its etymology. It plays back and forth among the religious, aesthetic, and sentimental uses of the word. George Eliot's form of inflation, of being filled with a god, is not any of these. It is a sideways transposition of them all, as realism is a mirror image of something which is not, strictly speaking, there. To put this another way, realism is like the act of coinage. It is like that sort of performative which stamps an image on paper or metal and so makes it pass current, makes it worth so much as currency.

There is no way of using literal, conceptual, notional, or doctrinal languages for this mirroring with a difference. Only the performative catachresis of a figurative expression, that comes like a mighty rushing wind in upon the soul and breaks it in two almost, will work. The impact of such language is like religious experience, or like falling in love, or like a force of nature, according to the quadruple equation linking art, nature, love, and religion throughout *Adam Bede*. The ground of the "like" in this analogical series running "A is like B is like C is like D" is no solid ontological *logos*. The ground is analogy or figure itself. The base of these analogies is analogy. This means, in spite of the claim to a solid ground in "reality," that realistic fiction brings groundless novelty into the social world. It brings, for example, my power to love my ugly neighbor. Realism inserts an infinite zero as multiplier or divisor into the circuit of the equation moving away from reality and back to it. This zero is something without ground or substance that nevertheless has power to make something happen. Its efficacy makes it dangerous, a force perhaps for good, perhaps for ill. In

this it is analogous to the way the same unpredictable energy of
human emotion and human dreaming, in the story proper, motivates
a Hetty Sorrel as well as a Dinah Morris, the bad woman as well
as the good.

The danger in performative figures almost surfaces in
the attempt, in the final paragraph, to discriminate among three
emotive attitudes: baseless idealism, cynical nihilism, and George
Eliot's realism. The attempt to discriminate reveals, in spite of itself,
a similarity. To try to erect barriers allowing a compartmentalization
brings into the open an impossibility of deciding what difference
there is among these three modes of valuing. There is a secret
equivalence in measuring among them which might be defined by
saying that any number multiplied by zero is zero, any number
divided by zero is infinity.

The final paragraph of the chapter is of great "interest,"
in the sense that it adds an increment to what has already been
said, clarifying it and undermining it at once. The last paragraph
seems at first a rather casual afterthought added to the main
argument in defense of realism. In fact, it is of great importance
as a revelation of the grounds, or rather the groundlessness, the
zero base, of that argument. It asserts an equivalence in the low
valuation given to the ugly real by "that lofty order of minds who
pant after the ideal," on the one hand, and by mean, narrow, selfish
natures, on the other. Both idealists and cynics join in finding
"real" people of no account: "For I have observed this remarkable
coincidence, that the select natures who pant after the ideal, and
find nothing in pantaloons or petticoats great enough to command
their reverence and love, are curiously in unison with the narrowest
and pettiest." These two kinds of disvaluers are in turn opposed
to George Eliot himself, who finds his neighbor of infinite account.
Nevertheless, this comes to the same thing, as the paragraph covertly
reveals. It makes the same sum, in the sense that both the low
valuation and the high are figurative measures of what, as the
chapter tells the reader over and over, are "in fact" ugly, stupid,
inconsistent people. To love such people is just as baseless as to
call them, as Mr. Gedge the pubkeeper did, "a poor lot." In fact

Mr. Gedge may be closer to an exact mirroring of people as Mary Ann Evans actually sees them, but Gedge's cynicism is also a baseless valuing as much as is George Eliot's loving reverence for commonplace people. The difference, all-important for Eliot, like a plus or minus sign before a zero, is that the positive evaluation is life-enhancing. It creates and sustains the human community on the base of those baseless fictions which are absolutely "needful" if there is to be a human community at all: "It is more needful that I should have a fiber of sympathy connecting me with that vulgar citizen."

All emotive evaluation is performative. It makes something happen which has no cause beyond the words which express it. Since my neighbor is "really" ugly, stupid, inconsistent, to view a woman as not worth loving unless she dies before you possess her (French cynical idealism, the cynicism of those who reject the real and pant after the ideal); to measure everything by the norm of a mean and narrow mind, like Mr. Gedge, and find it wanting ("A poor lot, sir, big and little, and them as comes for a go o' gin are no better than them as comes for a pint o' twopenny—a poor lot."); to love one's ugly neighbor, knowing he or she is ugly, like George Eliot—all three come to the same thing. They are in unison. They make the same sum in the sense that they give measures which are analogies lacking a solid base in any *logos*. There is more than simple opposition in the relation between the closed circuit economy of realism, on the one hand, the ugly mirroring the ugly and returning the ugly to the ugly, and, on the other hand, the infinite economy of genius, the beautiful (angels and Madonnas, prophets, sibyls) mirroring nothing but the inventive soul of its creator, flying off into the inane ideal without possibility of return. Realism also adds a fictive plus value, and Madonnas or angels also make us admire human motherhood and self-denying aspiration.

George Eliot discharges his conscience, pays off his obligation, by covertly admitting his kinship with the positions he rejects. Extremes meet in their common baselessness. The cynicism which measures all people by a zero and finds them all equally poor

comes to the same thing as the positive measure which gives my
neighbor an infinite value, so generating a resolution to do good,
to love him or her. It comes to the same thing yet comes to a very
different thing in its effects, which makes all the difference between
the maintenance and the dissolution of society. The cement of
society is the fiction that my ugly, stupid neighbor is lovable. *Adam
Bede* dramatizes in the story of its titular hero the dangers of too
hardheaded and clear-seeing a power of judgment. Even the most
charitable performative, however, has its dangers. The oscillation
generated by the impossibility of distinguishing categorically between
these two attitudes, the selfish and the unselfish, the cynical and
the charitable, is the pervasive rhythm of thought and feeling in
Adam Bede as a whole. It is dramatized in the secret identity and
yet infinite difference between Hetty and Dinah. It is dramatized in
the impossibility of deciding whether Adam's deluded love for Hetty
is a good thing or a bad thing: "He created the mind he believed
in out of his own, which was large, unselfish, tender" (*AB*, ch. 33).
It is mimed finally in the impossibility of deciding whether the "I"
who speaks in chapter 17 is Mary Ann Evans talking of the real,
historical, autobiographical world of her father, her home county,
and her childhood experience, or whether, as it must also be, it is
those transposed into the fictive voice of an invented male narrator
speaking of fictive events and valuing them in groundless figurative
exchanges moving back and forth from love to nature to art to
religion. It is both and so neither.

My reading of George Eliot's reading of his (or her) own
writing has revealed an unsettling rift between the knowledge that
writing gives in its resolute commitment to truthtelling, and the
power to love one's neighbor the truthtelling story is supposed to
give. This fissure is not too different, after all, from the gulf between
the epistemology of metaphor and the necessary moment of "ethicity," in Paul de Man's account of his "paradigmatic" text, Rousseau's *Julie*. I turn now to Anthony Trollope's reading of his writing
self in *An Autobiography* to see whether Trollope may form the
basis of an alternative paradigm for the ethics of reading.

CHAPTER FIVE

Self Reading Self: Trollope

> Le texte se garde, comme la loi. Il ne parle que de lui-même, mais
> alors de son non-identité à soi. Il n'arrive ni ne laisse arriver à lui-
> même. Il est la loi, fait la loi et laisse le lecteur devant la loi.
> ——Jacques Derrida,[1]

George Eliot's version of the ethics of reading (in that peculiar form of it in which an author reads himself or herself) culminates, in chapter 17 of *Adam Bede,* in a special form of unreadability the rhetorical or tropological name for which is catachresis. Though Eliot, both in the act of self-reading in *Adam Bede* and in the story itself, takes away all transcendent authority or extralinguistic grounding for the act of naming called catachresis, that does not keep her from being unable to read her own lesson. She commits again the error she denounces when she renames her ugly, stupid neighbors lovable. Such renaming is for her the essence of storytelling in the realistic novel. The novel makes us love our unlovable neighbors by naming them lovable. I turn now to Anthony Trollope's *An Autobiography,* one of the most important examples of self-reading in Victorian England, to see whether he may provide a different conception of the ethics of reading.

In *An Autobiography* Anthony Trollope turns back near the end of his life on his whole career as a novelist and reads himself and his work. *An Autobiography* is perhaps the most extraordinary revelation of the mode of production and dissemination of a large fictional *oeuvre* we have for the whole Victorian period. That period was in England a historical high point for the production of novels and for their fulfillment of an irreplaceable social function. Then more than at any other time before or since, it could be argued, novels provided readers with whatever it is that fiction does provide its readers—perhaps a chance to make in imagination "experiments in life," as George Eliot said; perhaps by a puissant enforcing or policing of a reigning ideology, as Foucaultian or Marxist critics are today in manifold ways arguing.

Any reader of *An Autobiography* is likely to see as important an early passage in which Trollope accounts for the way his novels came to be written. In this passage Trollope describes the writing of his novels as the transformation of a deplorable youthful habit of daydreaming. This transformation was a way out of childhood solitude into the society from which he had been excluded. "There can, I imagine," says Trollope, "hardly be a more dangerous mental practice; but I have often doubted whether, had it not been my practice, I should ever have written a novel. I learned in this way to maintain an interest in a fictitious story, to dwell on a work created by my own imagination, and to live in a world altogether outside the world of my own material life. In after years I have done the same,—with this difference, that I have discarded the hero of my early dreams, and have been able to lay my own identity aside."[2] Earlier in *An Autobiography* Trollope describes eloquently his miserable childhood at Harrow and Winchester as the child of an impecunious member of the professional middle class, a failed lawyer who could barely pay his son's bills at those fashionable schools, much less give him proper clothes or pocket money. In his account Trollope emphasizes two special sources of misery, his exclusion from the games of the other boys ("Of the cricket-ground or racket-court I was allowed to know nothing" [A, 14]), and his exclusion from the language of the others. He could not, he says, learn Latin and Greek, which were of course among the primary subjects taught (A, 35), and he was mute even in English when speech might have allowed him to right an injustice done him: "With all a stupid boy's slowness, I said nothing" (A, 5). Trollope defines his habit of daydreaming as substitute play, solitary play or play with himself, with an implicit sexual connotation also present in that phrase about the "dangerous mental practice": "I have explained, when speaking of my school-days, how it came to pass that other boys would not play with me. I was therefore alone, and had to form my plays within myself. Play of some kind was necessary to me then, as it has always been" (A, 36). In the transformation of the daydreams into novel-writing, the muteness of solitary reverie became externalized language, written down and transmissible to others. The focus on himself in his daydreams ("I was of course my own hero" [A, 37]) became the production of imaginary characters distinct from himself. When the novels were accepted by publishers, printed, sold, and read, Trollope entered into the social world from which he had been excluded. He got others, so to speak, to play *his* game, the game established by the rules and conventions of his novels.

Both in his account of his daydreams and in his account of the process later on of writing his novels, Trollope emphasizes the way his acts of imagination were rule-bound, made to submit to laws of internal consistency, continuity, probability, and moderation: "For weeks, for months, if I remember rightly, from year to year, I would carry on the same tale, binding myself down to certain laws, to certain proportions, and proprieties, and unities. Nothing impossible was ever introduced,—nor even anything which, from outward circumstances, would seem to be violently improbable" (A, 36–37); "But as I had made up my mind to undertake this second profession, I found it to be expedient to bind myself by certain self-imposed laws" (A, 102).

In the first quotation the laws are those within the daydream. In the second, the laws are those extraordinary rules whereby Trollope bound himself to write novels from five to eight o'clock every morning—at home or away from home, in his study or on the train or on shipboard—and bound himself to write two hundred and fifty words every fifteen minutes, a thousand words an hour, and so on. "Nothing surely," says Trollope, "is so potent as a law that may not be disobeyed. It has the force of the water-drop that hollows the stone" (A, 103). Is this "law," one might ask, purely "self-imposed," "self-wrought," as Kant would say, "autonomous" in the etymological sense of a private law for oneself, or is it in one way or another a response to some law beyond the self, a response to some categorical demand from the "law as such," a law simultaneously aesthetic and moral? That remains to be seen, but it may be said in anticipation that this is just the question on which all of Trollope's novels turn, as do the novels of Henry James, my topic in the last chapter here.

The process whereby daydreams became novels which were bought, read, and made Trollope well known, socially accepted, member of many London clubs, able to run (unsuccessfully) for Parliament, fits exactly, so it seems, Freud's paradigmatic formulation at the end of the twenty-third chapter of *Introductory Lectures on Psycho-Analysis* of the artwork as a means of attaining through fantasy (and through providing for the need of others for fantasy) satisfaction in the real world of the universal male desire for "honour, power, wealth, fame and the love of women." "[H]e has thus achieved," says Freud, "*through* his phantasy what originally he had acieved only *in* his phantasy—honour, power and the love of women."[3] An obvious question remains, however. It is also a question which occurs in a different way within Freud's own work.[4] Why, when Trollope had attained in the real world *through* fantasy what he had before only been able to attain *in* fantasy, did he not stop writing novels? The accounts he gives later on in *An Autobiography* of the mode of production of his novels will give a tentative answer to that question, though only a detailed reading of the novels themselves would confirm the hypothesis I shall propose.

My hypothesis is that what Trollope says about the production of his novels is incoherent. It is incoherent in the sense that it cannot be made to hang together logically as a single concept of the making and use of fiction. Trollope wants above all to say one thing, but in spite of himself he says another thing which subverts the claim he wishes to make for the nature and function of his novels.

On the one hand, Trollope goes to elaborate lengths to persuade his readers that his novels have a good moral effect because they return the same to the same, that is, they are modeled on social reality and reflect back to his readers themselves. "I do believe," he says,

> that no girl has risen from the reading of my pages less modest than she was before, and that some may have learned from them that modesty is a charm well worth preserving. I think that no youth has been taught that in falseness and flashness is to be found the road to manliness; but some may perhaps have learned from me that it is to be found in truth and a high but gentle spirit. Such are the lessons I have striven to teach; and I have thought that it might best be done by representing to my readers characters like them-selves,—or to which they might liken themselves." (A, 126–127).

About the particular morality Trollope wants to teach, with its resolute discrimination between the sexes (the "charm" of modesty for women, truth and manliness for men), I say nothing now. My interest is in the way this morality is to be taught by reflecting back to his readers characters like themselves or to whom in emulation they might liken themselves. The argument is not too different from George Eliot's defense of realism, except that in Trollope's case the function of realistic fiction is to give us fictional characters on whom to model ourselves, whereas for George Eliot it is a matter of presenting people like our neighbors and persuading us to love them. Trollope's theory of the novel, like George Eliot's, guarantees that his readers will get their money's worth when they buy *The Warden* or *Orley Farm.* The guarantee depends on the fact that the novels will have a constructive social function, namely to reinforce the ethical values of the middle-class readers for whom they are intended.

Trollope's stake in the efficient circulation of novels within society, returning the values of that society to itself (as in

the phrase "circulating library"), might find an analogy in his
vigorous efforts as a civil servant working for the post office to
make sure that letters sent all over England, Ireland, and the Empire,
would rapidly and cheaply reach their destinations:

> The object was to create a postal network which should catch all
> recipients of letters. . . . During those two years it was the ambition
> of my life to cover the country with rural letter-carriers. . . . I did
> . . . do my work, and can look back upon what I did with thorough
> satisfaction. I was altogether in earnest; and I believe that many a
> farmer now has his letters brought daily to his house free of charge,
> who but for me would still have had to send to the post-town for
> them twice a week, or to have paid a man for bringing them irregularly
> to his door (A, 76, 77, 79).

Trollope's energy and imagination as a civil servant were
caught by the project of an extremely rapid and efficient transfer
of information from place to place and from person to person
throughout England and its possessions. He was the inventor of
the pillar postbox. His novel-writing transferred that image of efficient
communication to the circulation of fictional characters and their
stories—from the real social world through the novelist and back
to society in the form of novels which were printed, published, paid
for, and read.

The essence of novel-writing (defining novel-writing as
this form of participation in the free circulation of regnant social
values) is for Trollope the production of characters, not of plots.
Characters in novels are "created personages impregnated with traits
of character which are known. To my thinking, the plot is but the
vehicle for all this" (A, 109). Characters in novels rearrange elements
of character which are already known to their readers. Such characters pay those readers back in their own coin, so to speak or,
to follow the image of impregnation, are children who bear a family
resemblance to the character traits of those who read the novels.
Coining is like impregnation in that it is the passing on of a
preexisting pattern. An invented character in a novel, to follow out
the metaphor, is like a new coin imprinted with insignia and in-

scriptions (the Queen's head or the motto of the garter, for example) which pass current in that society. Such a new coin can be put in circulation and will have recognizable value there. It will be homogeneous to the value system of the society within which it circulates, recognizable within it and measurable in worth by it, not heterogenous, incommensurate, and therefore inassimilable. Such coinage will ratify and be ratified by the standards of validity and worth it exemplifies. An essay in the *National Review* for January 1863, in fact employs such a commercial metaphor to describe the role of the characters in Trollope's novels in English society. "The characters are public property," said the *National Review,* and as a result Trollope has become "almost a national institution. . . . So great is his popularity, so familiar are his chief characters to his countrymen, so widespread is the interest felt about his tales, that they necessarily form part of the common stock-in-trade with which the social commerce of the day is carried on."[5] The formulation is testimony to Trollope's accomplishment of his aim: to make the characters in his novels a medium of social communication affirming and maintaining the values of that society.

The function of such characters, once they are produced and put in circulation, is ethical: "I have ever thought of myself as a preacher of sermons, and my pulpit as one which I could make both salutary and agreeable to my audience. . . . But the novelist, if he have a conscience, must preach his sermons with the same purpose as the clergyman, and must have his own system of ethics. If he can do this efficiently, if he can make virtue alluring and vice ugly, while he charms his reader instead of wearying him" (A, 126, 190), then he will have fulfilled his social function and can with a clear conscience enjoy the entry into society the writing of novels has obtained for him.

Many additional elements in Trollope's account of the way his novels were written and sold go to support this definition of novels as part of the restrained or closed economy of his society. In this economy everything has its value. The value of the most apparently heterogeneous items can be measured by the same standard: money. Everything of value enters into a circuit of production,

purchase, and consumption within which nothing alien or unac-
countable can ever be introduced. Among such additional elements
in Trollope's account of his novels is that notorious table toward
the end of *An Autobiography* in which Trollope lists exactly what
he was paid for each of his novels. He adds all the figures up in
a final accounting to make the grand total (by 1879) of 68,939
pounds, 17 shillings, and 5 pence, including 7,800 pounds for
"Sundries" (A, 312–313). The value of his novels can be measured
by the amount of money he has been paid for them, and Trollope
can congratulate himself on a job well done and adequately re-
munerated: "I look upon the result as comfortable, but not splendid"
(A, 314).

In congruence with this acceptance of a monetary measure of worth, Trollope is anxious to assure his readers that they
have got good value for their money, for example in repeated
assertions that he always provided his publishers with the exact
number of words promised, no more and no less, an exact full
measure of the commodity purchased. He repeatedly compares novel-
writing to a working-class (and preindustrial) occupation like shoemaking, in which there is a relatively easy measure of the value of
the commodity produced, and an easy measure of the amount of
labor which has gone into its production. It is or it is not a good
shoe, and so many hours of work have gone into its making. For
the idea that the writer should wait for inspiration Trollope has
nothing but scorn:

> There are those who would be ashamed to subject them-
> selves to such a taskmaster, and who think that the man who works
> with his imagination should allow himself to wait till—inspiration
> moves him. When I have heard such doctrine preached, I have hardly
> been able to repress my scorn. To me it would not be more absurd
> if the shoemaker were to wait for inspiration, or the tallow-chandler
> for the divine moment of melting. If the man whose business it is
> to write has eaten too many good things, or has drunk too much,
> or smoked too many cigars,—as men who write sometimes will do,—
> then his condition may be unfavourable for work; but so will be the
> condition of a shoemaker who has been similarly imprudent. . . .

Mens sana in corpore sano. The author wants that as does every
other workman,—that and a habit of industry. (A, 104, 105)

As can be imagined, such statements have hardly done
Trollope's reputation as a novelist much good over the years, though
his detractors have perhaps missed the odd combination of irony
and modesty in such passages in *An Autobiography,* along with the
somewhat overanxious desire to assimilate novel-writing into the
approved Victorian pattern of hard work at a socially useful job.
An uneasy conscience is part of the mixture of slightly defiant
assertion with which Trollope affirms that he has written his novels
in the same way that a shoemaker makes his shoes. Most of us,
even if we followed his recipe, could produce nothing at all so good
as *Orley Farm or The Last Chronicle of Barset* or *He Knew He
Was Right.* We would be more likely to learn in time how to make
a good shoe.

In a passage already quoted Trollope writes of the
"efficiency" with which a novel should combine pleasure and moral
instruction, so that his readers will get two for the price of one,
so to speak. Nothing could be more conventional, even banal, than
this expression of the standard of "utile et dulce." Trollope's
insistence on the economic aspect of this combination is, however,
less conventional. Trollope's willingness to assimilate his novels
completely into the enclosed economy of his society, where everything has its clear measure of worth, is indicated by his emphasis
on the efficiency with which they were produced, as well as by his
emphasis on the efficiency with which they do their work. If they
are valuable because they economically combine two social values,
pleasure and moral teaching, they were produced by a businesslike
application which manufactured so many words every quarter of an
hour with the efficiency of a factory worker on the production line
or of a shoemaker making shoes.[6]

This emphasis on the efficiency of the transmission,
through the novelist's conscience (and consciousness) back to his
readers, of what they already know, in a closed circuit exchanging
the same for the same, is, finally, indicated in Trollope's description

of the proper style for novels which have as their goal a rapid circulation within society. Such a style is one in which language effaces itself. In an efficient novel language is a pure transparent medium by means of which what is in the mind of the novelist is transmitted back to the minds of his readers, from which it originally came:

> His language must come from him as music comes from the rapid touch of the great performer's fingers; as words come from the mouth of the indignant orator; as letters fly from the fingers of the trained compositor; as the syllables tinkled out by little bells form themselves to the ear of the telegraphist. (A, 152)

> The language used should be as ready and as efficient a conductor of the mind of the writer to the mind of the reader as is the electric spark which passes from one battery to another battery. (A, 202)

In these figures the medium vanishes in its flawless working. Just as the little bells become instantly letters, the letters words, the words meaningful sentences, to the ear of the expert telegraphist, so Trollope's novels must in the end vanish into the circuit of communication they establish between society and an author who has by his writing triumphantly gained his end, conquered his initial solitude, and become thoroughly assimilated into his surrounding society. Trollope himself, as a separate person, a social misfit, has vanished into the community of his readers, just as, for example, his heroines disappear into their communities when at the end of his novels they marry and achieve fixed social roles. In a similar way Mr. Harding, by the end of *The Warden,* is no longer in the public eye, no longer the object of vehement attacks and defenses. When he resigns the wardenship he melts back into a social role in which he is accepted by everyone as rector of St. Cuthbert's and "not warden now, only precentor,"[7] as the last words of the novel affirm.

So much for one orientation of what Trollope says about novel-writing. I have been identifying the public and institutional side, so to speak, of Trollope's theory of the novel. It is the side Trollope apparently has the most stake in emphasizing and affirming.

He must affirm it in order to be able to assert with a clear conscience the positive role novel-writing has played in his entry into the society from which he had been so painfully excluded as a child. In the other direction, however, Trollope says, in spite of himself, as it were, something which goes against the grain of his official doctrine, something which undermines and subverts that doctrine. Here is one passage in which that counter-doctrine comes clearly into the open. Trollope here speaks of the rapidity with which his novels get written at times when he is free of household cares and the cares of his bureaucratic work at the Post Office, free also of the temptations of whist at his club. At first it may seem that what Trollope is saying here is no more than a reinforcement of the idea that the proper style of an efficient novel is one which transmits with transparent ease what is in the mind of the author into the mind of the reader. But more than that is being said. Here is the passage:

> I believe that the work which has been done quickest has been done the best. . . . How short is the time devoted to the manipulation of a plot can be known only to those who have written plays and novels;—I may say also, how very little time the brain is able to devote to such wearing work. There are usually some hours of agonising doubt, almost of despair,—so at least it has been with me,—or perhaps some days. And then, with nothing settled in my brain as to the final development of events, with no capability of settling anything, but with a most distinct conception of some character or characters, I have rushed at the work as a rider rushes at a fence which he does not see. (A, 150–151)

Here is something different from what I have found so far in Trollope's account of the production of his novels. It emerges not as something second that comes after the official and overt doctrine, assumed to be "first." It exists rather entwined with the "first" all along, though going counter to it and saying something which unravels it rather than forming with it a single stronger strand. In the passage just quoted the emphasis on spontaneity and speed is no longer simply the definition of a mode of efficiency in the production and transmission of character from author to reader. It says something about the way character is produced in the first place. That production, the passage suggests, is not the careful assemblage of "traits of character which are known," that is, known to both author and reader and therefore forming the preexisting basis of the circuit of exchange between them. It is rather the spontaneous and uncalculated "conception" of character within the imagination of the author. This conception is not even the result of constructive conscious thought. It comes out of nowhere as a kind of immaculate conception enabling the writing of the novel. The production of characters and of stories for those characters is a desperate act like that of a man riding at a fence he cannot see. Trollope speaks elsewhere in *An Autobiography* of his reckless wildness as a rider to hounds and of his many resulting falls: "Few have investigated more closely than I have done the depth, and breadth, and water-holding capacities of an Essex ditch" (A, 147). Riding to hounds, like whist, is one of those games of the others which the adult Trollope was allowed to play. Riding is not only an emblem for him, within his novels, of social life generally, but provides, as here, an analogy for that novel-writing which was a displacement of daydreaming. It was a substitute, that is, for what had substituted for playing the games of others when Trollope was a child. Like jumping a fence or a ditch, the production of character is not a matter of calculation or thought. It is a desperate act of putting pen to paper and seeing what words form themselves on the page without Trollope's premeditation as the actualization of that "most distinct conception of some character or characters" with which he has begun.

A few pages earlier Trollope had made this strange thoughtlessness of his act of novel-writing explicit: "I have never found myself thinking much about the work that I had to do till I was doing it. I have indeed for many years almost abandoned the effort to think, trusting myself, with the narrowest thread of a plot, to work the matter out when the pen is in my hand" (A, 134). "To work the matter out when the pen is in my hand": the pen, in this extraordinary sentence, seems to do the thinking for Trollope.

The reader will remember the discussion in the last chapter of a similar passage in George Eliot's *Adam Bede.* The pen, for George Eliot, or rather for his bad, unrealistic artist, does the thinking and is "conscious of a delightful facility."

In Trollope's case, on the other hand, there is no thinking at all involved in the matter. The pen is a tool like the hammer or awl of the shoemaker, and the production of novels is a form of handwork. In this work the conception of character takes place spontaneously through a skilled manipulation of the pen that has become so habitual that the pen no longer has to be consciously directed by the mind. This is parallel to the way the hands and tools of a skilled shoemaker fashion a shoe with expert speed while the mind of the shoemaker may be occupied with something else entirely, or be entirely blank. Or the workmanship involved may, according to another metaphor implicit in Trollope's terminology, be that women's work of spinning. As he produces his novels Trollope follows the narrowest thread of a plot, like Theseus threading his way through the baffling corridors of the labyrinth to safety along the line spun out from Ariadne's bobbin. Trollope cites a letter to him from Thackeray which speaks of "novel spinning" (A, 119), and Trollope himself argues that a consistency of beginning and end "should be kept in view as to every . . . string of action" (A, 120). His motto as a writer, *nulla dies sine lineâ,* defines the writing of novels as the continuous production of a line or thread of words flowing day by day out of the pen onto the paper and leading by an unbroken sequence from beginning to end, from the center of the labyrinth to the open air. In either case, whether writing novels is thought of as like shoemaking or as like spinning a thread, the characters so wrought seem to come magically from nowhere, out of the pen.

The sexual metaphor latent or not so latent in the term "conception," in the phrase "created personages impregnated with traits of character which are known," and in that image of the spontaneously creative pen is made even more explicit in a passage following the ones quoted above arguing that rapid unthinking composition is best. In reading this passage the reader may remember that passage in which Freud speaks of patients who find it impossible to write because they have unconsciously identified writing with a forbidden sexual act. The two are alike in that both involve the use of a cylindrical object from which a liquid flows.[8] Here is the passage in Trollope:

> When my work has been quickest done,—and it has sometimes been done very quickly—the rapidity has been achieved by hot pressure, not in the conception, but in the telling of the story. Instead of writing eight pages a day, I have written sixteen; instead of working five days a week, I have worked seven. . . . This has generally been done at some quiet spot among the mountains,—where there has been no society, no hunting, no whist, no ordinary household duties. And I am sure that the work so done has had in it the best truth and the highest spirit that I have been able to produce. At such times I have been able to imbue myself thoroughly with the characters I have had in hand. I have wandered alone among the rocks and woods, crying at their grief, laughing at their absurdities, and thoroughly enjoying their joy. I have been impregnated with my own creations till it has been my only excitement to sit with the pen in my hand, and drive my team before me at as quick a pace as I could make them travel. (A, 151–152)

In this extraordinary passage the sexual metaphor latent in the terminology of the "conception" of character comes more or less fully into open. Along with this comes into the open also the fact that the transformation of Trollope's habit of solitary daydreaming into the workmanlike production and selling of novels measured by so many pages manufactured through so many hours of work has by no means escaped from the dangerous conditions of that daydreaming. What Trollope says here goes against all his attempts to define novels as safely within the circuit of the exchange of the same for the same within society. The production of characters is rather an act of auto-affection and auto-fecundation in which Trollope, pen in hand, impregnates himself with his own creations. He doubles himself within himself into characters and into the creative consciousness which is the matrix for those characters. He thereby plays within himself the role of both male and female, going it alone, as they say, in an act in which the self becomes the imaginary selves the creative self has made out of nothing but its own powers of imagination, consciousness, or "conscience" (to use Trollope's key word for this self-begetting power of the mind). The result of this "hot pressure" of self-impregnation is a heightened state of emotion. His creativity produces an ecstasy in which Trollope is beside himself, so to speak. He cries, laughs, and enjoys all at once by way of the imaginary tears, laughter, and joy of the characters he has created. These have no authority other than himself and no other source than himself. The illicit or illegitimate birth of this strange act of auto-insemination is the text of the novel. This counterfeit production is then passed off as legitimate coin. It is put into circulation and achieves the results for Trollope of assimilation into society I have described. It is as though a man should grow rich through the manufacture of counterfeit coin so expertly made and so apparently genuine as never to be found out, since it causes no more than an imperceptible inflation in the general currency. Behind Trollope's apparent success in becoming like the others by making simulacra of the others in his novels, he remains as solitary, as alien, and as inassimilable as ever. He remains an island of heterogeneity which cannot be measured by publicly accepted standards of value. His novels too are secretly like himself in their incommensurability with those standards.

In his account of the writing and reception of his first successful novel, *The Warden,* Trollope mentions the way two characters, Archdeacon Grantly and Tom Towers, were praised for their verisimilitude, for their accurate representation of real people in the real social world. In the case of Tom Towers, the journalist in *The Warden,* he was accused, in fact, of copying exactly a real member of the staff of the London *Times.* No, says Trollope, in both cases the character was not based on any direct observation at all. It was rather the product of free invention by his moral conscience or consciousness. The characters were the product, that is, of that process of self-induced and baseless creation he defines according to the metaphor of auto-impregnation:

I have been often asked in what period of my early life I had lived so long in a cathedral city as to have become intimate with the ways of a Close. I never lived in any cathedral city,—except London, never knew anything of any Close, and at that time had enjoyed no particular intimacy with any clergyman. My archdeacon, who has been said to be life-like, and for whom I confess that I have all a parent's fond affection, was, I think, the simple result of an effort of my moral consciousness. It was such as that, in my opinion, that an archdeacon should be,—or, at any rate, would be with such advantages as an archdeacon might have; and lo! an archdeacon was produced, who has been declared by competent authorities to be a real archdeacon down to the very ground. And yet, as far as I can remember, I had not then ever spoken to an archdeacon. I have felt the compliment to be very great. The archdeacon came whole from my brain after this fashion. (A, 80)

At that time, living away in Ireland, I had not even heard the name of any gentleman connected with the *Times* newspaper, and could not have intended to represent any individual by Tom Towers. As I had created an archdeacon, so had I created a journalist, and the one creation was no more personal or indicative of morbid tendencies than the other. If Tom Towers was at all like any gentleman then connected with the *Times,* my moral consciousness must again have been very powerful. (A, 86)

Trollope's self-reading in *An Autobiography* is, I have tried to show, fundamentally self-contradictory. He wants to show how the writing of novels was a means of legitimate entry into society. He wants to show that his novels are moral in the sense of affirming the values of that society. He wants to show that his readers have got their money's worth when they have purchased his novels. In spite of himself he shows the opposite. He shows that he has perpetrated a kind of fraud, that he has secretly undermined the values of his society, and that for their shillings his readers have purchased books which are for that reason dangerous or subversive.

I hope to show in another place that the drama of *An Autobiography* is repeated in another way by the drama of the novels themselves. The novels are all versions of an ever-renewed, ever-unsuccessful attempt to demonstrate that moments of moral decision on the part of Trollope's invented characters are securely grounded in a demonstrable right to act as they do act. Two examples of this out of almost innumerable moments of moral choice in Trollope's novels are Mr. Harding's decision to resign the wardenship in *The Warden* and Nora Rowley's decision not to accept Mr. Glascock's proposal of marriage in *He Knew He Was Right.* Instead of showing that these decisions, and others like them, are solidly grounded, Trollope demonstrates again and again that the sought-for solid ground slips away and vanishes. Moral decision may therefore be an ungrounded act of self-affection like Trollope's act of creating characters out of nothing but his unaided "moral consciousness." "I am thought in the wrong by all those whom I have consulted in the matter;" writes the Warden in his formal letter of resignation to his friend the Bishop, "I have very little but an inward and unguided conviction of my own to bring me to this step" (W, 236). Far from providing examples of the bridge between the law as such and the application of that law to a particular case of moral decision which Kant suggests narration or storytelling should be, Trollope's novels repeat or double the fissure between general law and particular law they are meant to allow the reader securely to cross. Beneath one deep a deeper deep still opens.

Trollope's novels put their readers (and Trollope himself) in the unhappy situation that Samuel Johnson says a man who claims to have an "inner light" puts those around him. Johnson, says Boswell, viewed the "inward light" as "a principle utterly incompatible with social or civil security." "If a man (said he,) pretends to a principle of action of which I can know nothing, nay, not so much as that he has it, but only that he pretends to it; how can I tell what that person may be prompted to do? When a person professes to be governed by a written ascertained law, I can then know where to find him."[9] A man who claims to have an inner light and to act on the basis of "conscience" in the traditional sense of the self within the self, the still small voice of God within the soul, may have that basis or he may not. It is impossible to tell. And yet, as Kant persuasively argues, all truly ethical decision must be based on such a response to an unconditional demand. The demand is made by the law as such on the one who decides. His decision in response to the demand must be free of all calculation as to the result based on fear or inclination. All Trollope's novels hover around the impossibility, in the end, of distinguishing between apparently solidly grounded ethical choice, such as Trollope's creation of characters through acts of moral consciousness, or Nora's refusal of Mr. Glascock because she "must" refuse him, or the Warden's decision to resign and, on the other hand, a disastrous and destructive ethical decision. An example of the latter is Hugh Trevelyan's conviction that his wife has betrayed him, in *He Knew He Was Right*. Trevelyan knows he is right, or thinks he knows. He goes through all the proper interior motions. He too responds to an imperative ethical exigency in a way like that leading for characters such as Nora Rowley or Septimus Harding to valid moral action. But he is wrong. Or rather, it is impossible to know for sure that he is not as right, or as wrong, as the others. The ground in neither case can be confronted directly and ascertained, as could a written law. Though one might hope that novels, since they are made of language, would provide that "written ascertained law" which Johnson demands, they do no more than demonstrate again and again the absence or unattainability of the law. In Trollope's novels, the moral law, the law as such, is as unattainable, as impossible ever to confront and to formulate in so many words, as it is for Kafka's man from the country, in "Vor dem Gesetz," to get a positive response to his humble and obedient request for direct access to the law.

Trollope found this situation intolerable. His obsessive writing of novels was continued well beyond any economic necessity and beyond his attainment of the social acceptance he had sought through writing. The secret motivation for this, it may be, was an attempt to write a novel which would assuage his need for a written ascertained moral law. He too, like his characters, sought secure possession of the grounds of moral decision through an indubitable entry into the law as such. Instead of that, his novels, as he progresses from one to another, enter more and more deeply into an understanding of what it means to define the human condition as separation from secure grounds of moral choice. One example, though only one among many, is his admirably full treatment of Louis Trevelyan in *He Knew He Was Right*. That novel is generated out of one of Trollope's most unsettling and powerful conceptions of character. But I defer a fuller discussion of Trollope's novels to another time and to another place. I turn now to my final example of an author reading himself, perhaps the most extraordinary example of all my three, Henry James' preface to *The Golden Bowl*.

CHAPTER SIX

Re-Reading Re-Vision:
James and Benjamin

. . . l'instance éthique travaille la littérature au corps.
                                                    Jacques Derrida[1]

At the end of that admirably eloquent act of verbal creation, the prefaces to the New York edition of his work, Henry James speaks of the way writing can be an ethical act, part of conduct. Writing is a use of words to make something happen for which the writer must, or may, take responsibility and continue to take responsibility by acknowledging the "connection," as the father of an illegitimate child may nevertheless acknowledge it. Plato, one remembers, spoke of writing (as opposed to living speech) as a fatherless child wandering the world without relations. James' claim, in this last paragraph of all of his prefaces, is just the opposite. Writing is not only a field for doing, but a field in which responsibility for the effects of doing may be conspicuously and stringently kept in view.

My question throughout this book has been whether reading can also be an ethical act, a performance, part of the conduct

of life, with its own measurable effects and consequent responsibilities. My focus throughout has been on only one corner of this
field, those places where we can see an author reading himself or
herself. Writers, however, are in one way or another exemplary
readers, perhaps even of themselves. Such passages, I have implicitly
claimed, are therefore exemplary for interrogation of the question
of the ethics of reading. In following through one small arc of the
trajectory of that prodigious act of re-reading as re-vision which is
recorded in James' "Prefaces," I want to make James' text my law.
I want to follow what he says with entire fidelity and obedience,
to see whether what he says about the ethics of reading may be
made the basis of a universal legislation. This book has explored
various acts of self-reading, in Kant, de Man, Eliot, Trollope, and
now James. It has also been itself all along an example of what it
is about. I have performed acts of reading of my own which are
both responses to an ethical demand made by the texts I have read
and at the same time ethical acts themselves which may have
performative force in their turn on my readers. This power of acts
of writing and then of reading to engender a limitless chain of
further such acts is in fact one theme of that last paragraph of all
in the last preface, the preface to *The Golden Bowl.* To that I now
turn.

        Let me look closely at James' own words, taking them
as the things I, for the moment, most respect. "The whole conduct
of life," says James, "consists of things done, which do other things
in their turn." Life, according to James here, is primarily doing,
not knowing, and not passively appreciating. Praxis, ethics, here
takes precedence over both epistemology and aesthetics, as indeed
I think in the end it always does for James, as perhaps it does in
the end also for Kant. Doing, moreover, for James, does not stop
with the initial act, but goes on doing and causing other things to
be done, in an endless chain of consequences. This might give
anyone pause on the brink of even the most apparently trivial act
or mode of conduct. Who knows what it might cause to happen
and where its further effects and relations might stop? If I make a

trivial promise intending not to keep it, the whole fabric of trust and responsibility in society is in danger of being unwoven.

In a passage often quoted from the preface to *Roderick Hudson,* James affirms that "really, universally, relations stop nowhere."[2] Here again, in the preface to *The Golden Bowl,* he emphasizes the interconnection, the hanging together, the continuity, for bliss or for bale, of the moral life. Something done can never be undone. All our doings, along with what their results cause to be done in their turn, form one indestructible web. In this web there are no gaps. The law of this social fabric is openness, a publicity which brings everything out in the open and keeps it there. As the conduct of life consists of things done which do things in their turn, "just so," says James, "our behaviour and its fruits are essentially one and continuous and persistent and unquenchable, and so, among our innumerable acts, are no arbitrary, no senseless separations" (P, 347). Moral acts, things done, left to themselves, neither die and disappear, nor fall apart from one another. They hang together and continue to hang together. If there come to be gaps, those gaps are the product of our own free choices to make them. Therefore they are not senseless. They are full of human sense. They have that particular form of sense which is betrayal by disowning, as when a father or mother disowns a child. This is what in fact happens to Maisie in James' *What Maisie Knew,* to cite one example of the way what is *in* James' novels as theme and action echoes the action performed *by* the book itself. The book itself is a thing James does by the way he puts things and as an act of narration by the narrator within the fiction of the book, another thing done, or "put." Exploration of those analogies, however, must wait for another occasion. The thing before me now is what James says about his own acts of writing and reading. I have taken responsibility for accounting primarily for those.

A play on those words "do," "thing," and "put" forms the transition in James' formulation from doing in general to that particular form of doing which is writing. Between conduct in the ordinary sense and the act of writing there are differences but no separations. "To 'put' things," says James "is very exactly and responsibly and interminably to do them. Our expression of them, and the terms on which we understand that, belong as nearly to our conduct and our life as every other feature of our freedom; these things yield in fact some of its most exquisite material to the religion of doing" (P, 347). The "religion of doing" here, I take it, refers not only to our American worship of pragmatic action as the thing most measurable and of value, but also suggests that doing is somehow a response to a demand or call, like a religious vocation. Doing is something that binds or ties us, as the etymology of the word "religion" implies, and as James seems to have remembered in the sentence following the one with the phrase about the "religion of doing" when he speaks of "the tie that binds us" to what we have written. Doing, including that form of doing performed with a pen or a typewriter or by oral dictation, involves an "I must" which is born of respect for the law, though what law it is James respects in writing or in re-reading remains to be seen. At the same time writing, like ethical action in general, is for James, as for Kant, a product of our freedom. It is free and bound at the same time.

The exact way that writing is doing is carried by the play on those three words I have mentioned. "Put" is an active verb, without doubt part of the vocabulary of doing, as when I say I put fruit in the refrigerator, or put money in the bank, or win a medal at the shot put. To "put" things in writing, however, is to transform those things into words, to express them or represent them, as when we say, "That's one way of putting it."

"Things" here does not mean only objects, like that fruit or that shot which the athlete "puts." It resonates with the full complexity of its meaning as a gathered complexity of human intercourse, as in the Germanic "thing" or legislative assembly, or as in what James elsewhere in this preface calls the "matter" of a story, as when we say "the matter of Rome" or "the matter of Troy," meaning the things narrated in the story. At the same time "thing" is a name for something all that surface complexity hides, or only obscurely reveals. The thing is what James calls, in two story titles, "the real thing" or "the right real thing" or what he hailed at the moment of his death as "the distinguished thing at last." Heidegger in "Das Ding" and Derrida in *Signéponge/Signsponge* have sought to define the elusive residuum we name "the thing." To " 'put' things" is, it may be, to enter into a transaction with that real thing behind the human things narrated and to respond to an obscure demand for narration made by that "real thing." The "thing" demands that it be respected by being put in words, so becoming a doing which may do other "things" in its turn, as James says.

Putting things in words, then, is an act of memory. It is narration as memorial in the sense of a preservative gathering or "recollection." In that word "recollection" memory and "thing" converge in a doing of things with words. The artist narrator of James' story "The Real Thing" ends his memorial record of a strange episode in his life which has damaged his art by saying: "I'm content to pay the price—for the memory." The doing of the thing, in this case, is the composition of its written record or memorial inscription, the record or accounting of the price paid for the value banked in the memory.

Of a great writer, who knows how to put things in words, we say that his things are really "done." They have finish, wholeness, and rounded completeness. A writer knows how to do things with words. So James praises Conrad, in a review of *Chance,* for being "absolutely alone as a votary of the way to do a thing that shall make it undergo the most doing."[3] Just how a good writer knows how to do things with words only a reading in detail of James' stories and novels could show. It has something to do with the analogy between the use James makes of the real-life donnée or germ of his stories and the act of renunciation or "not getting anything out of it for oneself" which universally forms the climactic moral decision and act of the protagonists of those stories. Only those acts of transformation and of renunciation liberate a glimpse of the "thing" behind "things." Here James wants to go on from his claim that "putting" things in words is "doing" them to claim further that this odd form of doing in fact has a "marked advantage" over other forms of doing in the real world of society

and history. One might think of putting things in words as rather
withdrawing them from circulation by changing them into words
and storing them up on the library shelves as recollection, as
narratives in the past tense, but James wants to deny this. The
expression of the "marked advantage" writing has over doing takes
the form of a chiasmus.

"Doing" in the ordinary sense of ethical action enters
directly into the social world and has effects of power there which
may be thought of as almost material, or are in fact material, as
in acts of violence or sexual acts. The latter in the form of adulterous
liaisons form the obscure (or not so obscure) background of most
of James' fiction, for example of *The Portrait of a Lady, The Aspern
Papers, What Maisie Knew,* or *The Golden Bowl.* Copulation is a
thing done with a vengeance. Nevertheless, such doings escape the
further power of the doer. They may even vanish without a trace,
so that we cannot own up to them even if we would.

Writing, on the other hand, is impalpable in its effects.
The name for those effects, at least the initial ones, is "reading,"
though alas a book can have not insignificant effects by hearsay
on those who have never read it and will never read it. Until a
book is read, one might think, it can have no "effect" at all, unless
it is used as a missile or falls on the head of someone who walks
by the shelf on which it is stored, but everyone knows of cases
where someone has a strong opinion about a book he or she has
not so much misread as not read at all and acts on the basis of
that opinion. The book is detached from its author and wanders
here and there by itself in the world, having such unpredictable
effects as it does have when it is read or misread, and even when
it is not read at all. On the other hand, the fact that writing leaves
tangible traces, namely the words on the page, means that the
author is free to go on owning up to his responsibility for what
he has done. And surely the legitimate effects of a book come about
when someone reads it. If the thing done by being put in words
can have its legitimate effect only through acts of reading, the
renewed affirmation of responsibility for things done in this way by

the perpetrator of such deeds can be nothing other than an act of re-reading, such as that prodigious act of re-reading, James' prefaces.

James' expression of the way writing is part of conduct takes, then, the form of a chiasmus which articulates the paradox that where we seem more responsible we are bound by a necessity which makes us in fact irresponsible, while where we are most free, untied, we are able to be more responsible, or are in fact, whether we will or not, responsible, since it is open to us to take responsibility or not. We are not bound by a necessity which frees us from responsibility. Here is James' admirably eloquent expression of this paradox. It is his ultimate formulation in the prefaces of the ethics of writing as an ethics of reading and re-reading. James' prose here has a grave and measured solemnity, a mixture of the colloquial and oratorical, which belongs to a peculiarly American tradition of moral reflection, the tradition, for example, of Emerson:

> Our literary deeds enjoy this marked advantage over many of our acts, that, though they go forth into the world and stray even in the desert, they don't to the same extent lose themselves; their attachment and reference to us, however strained, needn't necessarily lapse—while of the tie that binds us to *them* we may make almost anything we like. We are condemned, in other words, whether we will or no, to abandon and outlive, to forget and disown and hand over to desolation, many vital or social performances—if only because the traces, records, connexions, the very memorials we would fain preserve, are practically impossible to rescue for that purpose from the general mixture. We give them up even when we wouldn't—it is not a question of choice. Not so on the other hand our really "done" things of this superior and more appreciable order—which leave us indeed all licence of disconnexion and disavowal, but positively impose on us no such necessity. Our relation to them is essentially traceable, and in that fact abides, we feel, the incomparable luxury of the artist. It rests altogether with himself not to break with his value, not to "give away" his importances. Not to *be* disconnected, for the tradition of behaviour, he has but to feel that he is not; by his lightest touch the whole chain of relation and responsibility is reconstituted. Thus if he is always doing he can scarce, by his own measure, ever have done. All of which means for him conduct with

a vengeance, since it is conduct minutely and publicly attested. (A, 347-348)

The reader will see the rhythm of James' thought here, the way the elements in question shift from one side of the ledger of the accounting, changing their places and values. Where we are apparently most bound, that is in real acts, "vital or social performances," we are most free, free because the absence of traces, records, memorials of what we have done means necessarily disconnection, disowning, forgetting. We cannot remember and be responsible even if we would, since these acts, or rather this single act in one, memory as owning up, depends, so it seems, on the persistence of records, traces. Writing, considered as an act, has the inestimable advantage that the traces of it remain. This means that we are always free to reaffirm our allegiance to what we have written, even though we have all license of disconnection and disavowal too, license not so much to say "I did not write that," as to say, "I no longer believe that," or "I would not write it that way now," perhaps in response to a higher demand of some kind against which what we have written is now measured. Such disavowal is like a promise we do not keep. On the other hand, nothing is easier than to keep the promise an earlier piece of writing implicitly made. We have but to *feel* the responsibility and the whole chain of responsibility, ownership, and connection is instantly reestablished, by that lightest touch. Freedom makes for connection and responsibility; necessity for disconnection, divorce, and irresponsibility, as the three main elements in James' formulation, along with their negatives, are shifted from one side to the other around the major opposition between an act which leaves no traces, or may leave no traces, for example a secret act of adultery, and an act which consists in making traces, an act which is therefore fundamentally and intrinsically memorial, that is, an act of writing.

But how in fact does that secondary act of reaffirmation, that lightest touch which reconstitutes the chain, take place? If a distinguishing feature of things done, whether of the ordinary kind of vital or social performances or of that special subset which are

acts of writing, is that they "do other things in their turn," in the
case of writing this can only occur when the things done in writing
are read. A book stored on the library shelf causes nothing whatsoever to happen, except as it gives food to worms and cockroaches,
or except as it causes those illegitimate effects of hearsay I mentioned
above. Only when it is read does something more happen that the
writer might be willing to acknowledge, for example when you or
I read the preface to *The Golden Bowl* or *The Golden Bowl* itself.

Among those acts of reading are those of the author
by himself. Or rather these are more properly acts of re-reading,
since the author presumably read what he wrote as he wrote it.
That light touch which reconstitutes the chain can be nothing but
an explicit or implicit act of reading. This reading is a secondary
act of memory and ratification of the earlier contract or promise:
"I wrote that and I own up to it." James' prefaces as a whole are
the secondary traces and memorials, traces over the original traces,
of such an act of re-reading. The preface to *The Golden Bowl* takes
this topic of what happened to James in the "reperusal" of his
work as the special and climactic region of James' reflection. Here,
for example, he speaks of re-reading as a care for his books almost
like combing or grooming a domestic animal or pet: "The blest
good stuff, sitting up, in its myriad forms, so touchingly responsive
to new care of any sort whatever, seemed to pass with me a delightful
bargain, and in the fewest possible words. 'Actively believe in us
and then you'll see!'—it wasn't more complicated than that, and
yet it was to become as thrilling as if conditioned on depth within
depth. I saw therefore what I saw, and what these numerous pages
record, I trust, with clearness" (p. 341). The first promise, that in
the writing of the books in the first place, leads to a second contract
or bargain, one with a promise on both sides. If he re-reads with
fidelity and belief, the "blest good stuff" promises that he'll have
visions, deep visions, depth within depth, a regular *mise en abîme*
of seeing.

What actually happens to James when he accepts the
contract to re-read, renews the responsibility for what he has written?

It would seem that, as with any other reader, his primary responsibility is entire fidelity to the text. He must make the text his law,
as I began by saying I am trying to do in my acts of reading.
James, however, in an extraordinary series of paragraphs on re-
reading as re-vision which just precedes the passage about the
touching response of the blest good stuff to his renewed care,
testifies to quite a different experience of what his things done cause
to be done in their turn. To this surprising and unexpected testimony
I turn now as my final example of the ethics of reading in the form
it takes when an author reads himself.

    James has been talking about the "illustrations" for the
New York edition, those admirable photographs by Alvin Langdon
Coburn. He has argued in an intricate series of metaphors which
there is not space or time to discuss here that illustrations for
novels are acceptable only if the illustrations represent not some
scene or persons in the novel but, strangely, what the novel represents, something behind or deep within the text, the "matter" to
which both novel and picture allude: "His own [the writer's] garden,
however, remains one thing, and the garden he has prompted the
cultivation of at other hands becomes quite another; which means
that the frame of one's own work no more provides a place for
such a plot than we expect flesh and fish to be served on the same
platter" (P, 332). No "surf and turf" for James. It is a matter of
territorial dominion, and James jealously guards *his* "turf" from
invasion by works in another medium, so that his words may have
freely their own intrinsic "effect of illustration" (P, 331) without
elbowing or competition. Coburn's photographs, therefore, are "images, always confessing themselves mere optical symbols or echoes,
expressions of no particular thing in the text, but only of the type
or idea of this or that thing" (P, 333). The type or idea of a thing,
one may hazard, is the "real thing."

    Something like the same elusive concept of a side-by-
side representation of something beyond either version underlies
James' extraordinary account of what happened when he system-
atically re-read his novels and stories for the New York edition.
The figure he uses is once more of a spatial expanse, but this now

expresses not a garden plot to be cultivated. It is rather a blank
field of "matter" to be traversed. The implications of this figure
are odd, and James' exact terms must be scrutinized closely for
their strange implications for what I am calling the ethics of reading.
For his recent productions, James says, the act of re-reading was
an experience of grateful consent. His present footsteps fell naturally
into the old ones, as when we walk again in our footprints left in
a field of snow. Not so with his earlier works, where the experience
was rather like that of trying, unsuccessfully, to fit one's stride in
the footprints left by some other walker taller or shorter, in any
case with a different pace:

> To re-read in their order my final things . . . has been
> . . . to become aware . . . that the march of my present attention
> coincides sufficiently with the march of my original expression; that
> my apprehension fits, more concretely stated, without effort or strug-
> gle, certainly without bewilderment or anguish, into the innumerable
> places prepared for it. As the historian of the matter sees and speaks,
> so my intelligence of it, as a reader, meets him halfway, passive,
> receptive, appreciative, often even grateful; unconscious, quite bliss-
> fully, of any bar to intercourse, any disparity of sense between us.
> Into his very footprints the responsive, the imaginative steps of the
> docile reader that I consentingly become for him all comfortably sink;
> his vision, superimposed on my own as an image in cut paper is
> applied to a sharp shadow on a wall, matches, at every point, without
> excess or deficiency. This truth throws into relief for me the very
> different dance that the taking in hand of my earlier productions was
> to lead me; the quite other kind of consciousness proceeding from
> *that* return. Nothing in my whole renewal of attention to these things,
> to almost any instance of my work previous to some dozen years
> ago, was more evident than that no such active, appreciative process
> could take place on the mere palpable lines of expression—thanks
> to the so frequent lapse of harmony between my present mode of
> motion and that to which the existing footprints were due. It was,
> all sensibly, as if the clear matter being still there, even as a shining
> expanse of snow spread over a plain, my exploring tread, for appli-
> cation to it, had quite unlearned the old pace and found itself naturally
> falling into another, which might sometimes indeed more or less

agree with the original tracks, but might most often, or very nearly,
break the surface in other places. (P, 335–336)

The two main images here, that of the cut paper superimposed on a shadow and that of the double line of footprints
in the snow, are similar but by no means identical in their implications. Since what is expressed here can, it seems, be expressed
only in images, not in translucent concepts, each image must be
looked at sharply for what it tells the reader. The image of the
image in cut paper superimposed on a shadow is odd because it
reverses what one would expect or at any rate what I would expect
as the order of priority. Rather than saying his vision as reader fits
the one presented by the text his earlier self (now spoken of as a
"he") wrote, James gives the priority to his present vision. What
is remarkable is not that what he sees now fits so well what he
wrote then, but that what he sees now was so exactly anticipated
by what he wrote then. His present vision is the standard of
measurement, not, as one would expect when it is a question of
an act of reading, the text to which the reader should submit as
to his sovereign law, the source of his knowledge, the command
to his action.

James' figure is of that old practice of making a silhouette
of a human face or figure by cutting paper to match its sharp
shadow on a wall. The vision, figure, or shape made by the work
is like one's own shadow on the wall, not, so it seems, a vision of
anything about the wall itself. The old text is the artifice to be
measured for validity by its correspondence to his present living
vision, the real shadow on the wall: "his vision, superimposed on
my own as an image in cut paper is applied to a sharp shadow on
a wall, matches, at every point, without excess or deficiency."

At this point in his interpretation the reader of James
reading himself may ask, perhaps in some exasperation, "vision of
what?" The other master image of the paragraph gives the answer,
again a surprising one, at least to me, in part because it seems to
contradict the image of the silhouette on the wall. The "vision" is
not of something generated by the text, nor is it of something

subjective, the artist's private vision, which the text reports and which a reader, even James as a later reader of the work of his earlier self, has access to by way of the text, nor is it a vision of real events, people, social laws, or the germ story behind the fiction about which James has so much to say in the prefaces. No. The vision is of what James calls "the clear matter" of the story, that is, it is a vision of the wall itself, in one image, or of the expanse of shining snow, in the other. It is a vision of that against which both the shadow and the silhouette are projected. Or, in the other image, it is a vision of that undifferentiated field across which he walks either in the first written version or in the "re-vision," which is James' name for the act of re-reading his earlier writings. The story itself is a patterned or differentiated representation of the unpatterned and undifferentiated, the clear matter in the sense of a field without marks or discriminations.

This is an exceedingly curious notion of what a narration narrates, and just how the line of footprints or the silhouette can be said to be an accurate report, account, or representation of the ground on which it is inscribed is puzzling, to say the least. But there are more curious features yet to what James says. If the matter, that field of shining unmarked snow, is at the same time the "matter" of the story in the sense that one speaks of underlying intrigue or archetypal fable, the footprints in the snow, as opposed to the synchronic image of the shadow cast on the wall, suggest a temporal progress from here to there, like the "march" of a story. Each footprint might be thought of as corresponding to a word, a phrase, or an episode, as the writer traces out a trajectory across the untrodden "matter," or to use another of James' words for it, the "thing" of which the story is the narrative, relation, or written account. If the first writing is a species of "vision" of this "shining expanse of snow," or in James' admirable phrase for it later, "fields of light" (P, 341), the later re-reading is a "revision," but not in the sense of re-writing. James says the idea of re-writing terrified him. He found it impossible to imagine, much less to do: "What re-writing might be was to remain—it has remained for me to this hour—a mystery" (P, 339). It might be noted in passing that this sentence is more than a little disingenuous and misleading. There are in fact many crucial changes in the texts of his works provided by James for the New York edition, a word here, a phrase there, which may make much difference in meaning between the first version and the second. Nevertheless, James means here "re-vision" in the sense of "re-vision," re-reading as seeing again the "thing" behind the text. "To revise," says James, "is to see, or to look over, again—which means in the case of a written thing neither more nor less than to re-read it" (P, 338–339). As I have said, James uses the word "thing" with a complexity of doubled and redoubled meanings that is analogous to the meanings it has for Heidegger in "Das Ding" or *Die Frage nach dem Ding,* or for Derrida in *Signéponge/Signsponge* and elsewhere. Here is an example. Thing means, for James too, thing as object. A "written thing" is a book or manuscript, a thing like any other thing, an object one holds in one's hand. A "written thing" means also the account of a "thing" in the ancient sense of a gathering of people for a deliberation or negotiation, as the people in James' *The Golden Bowl* gather around the "thing" that most concerns them all, the hidden adultery of Charlotte and Prince Amerigo, the incestuous love of Maggie and her father. "Thing," finally, is the thing behind those things, thing as matter in the sense of a shining expanse of snow spread over a field, something both revealed and hidden, traduced, by the pattern of footprints impressed one by one across it.

Both James' images imply a freedom in the writer to do as he likes, to cast his own shadow on the wall, to cut the paper to any pattern made by that shadow, in one image; to move freely across the shining snow, making now one set of footprints, now another, in the other image. Just such freedom, however, is what James' experience of re-reading as re-vision categorically denies. The experience of trying unsuccessfully to walk in footprints made in the snow by someone else is unpleasant enough. It is even more difficult than making one's own new tracks across a trackless expanse. One makes every effort to make one's pace fit, since it would be much easier to walk in the old footprints than to make

new ones, but it does not work. The distance between one footprint
and another is too great or too small. One's muscles soon begin
to ache intolerably; one's feet begin to stumble. What James describes
is in a way even worse: the experience of discovering that one's
own mode of walking no longer fits an earlier one: "my exploring
tread had quite unlearned the old pace and found itself naturally
falling into another."

It might seem that what James is saying here is that
the passage of time has given him stronger legs, so to speak, so
that he has a longer stride, but this is not in fact what he says.
The necessity, he seems to be saying, comes from the other direction,
from the shining expanse of matter itself. It comes, I suggest, by
a species of imposition not unlike the effect of the hidden and
forever unattainable moral law on Kant's hypothetical maker of a
lying promise who discovers that he can will the lie but not a
universal law justifying lying promises. Here is James' formulation
of this strange experience of a coercion by something, the clear
matter, the "thing," that looks as if it were open to any mode of
traversal and were incapable of imposing any sort of coercion on
my freedom to walk where I like. "What was thus predominantly
interesting to note, at all events," says James, "was the high
spontaneity of these deviations and differences, which became thus
things not of choice, but of immediate and perfect necessity: necessity
to the end of dealing with the quantities in question at all" (P,
336). The reader should remember what James is naming with this
characteristically extravagant figure, that is, the experience of re-
reading his own earlier things. To re-read is to be forced by an
irresistible necessity that is not in the text he once wrote and now
re-reads, but appears to come from the matter that text represented
in a way he now finds inadequate. But if he is coerced, he is
strangely, also free.

In either case the experience of re-reading, like Kant's
description of the ethical man's relation to the moral law as such,
is not only absolutely necessitated either to agree or not to agree
with the old footprints, but also and at the same time is the
exhilarating experience of a spontaneity that James compares to a

specific philosophical or even religious experience, namely "a sudden large apprehension of the Absolute." Here are James' words for this: "No march, accordingly, I was soon enough aware, could possibly be more confident and free than this infinitely interesting and amusing *act* of re-appropriation; shaking off all shackles of theory, unattended, as was speedily to appear, with humiliating uncertainties, and almost as enlivening, or at least as momentous, as, to a philosophic mind, a sudden large apprehension of the Absolute" (P, 336). Re-reading is an act, an act of re-appropriation. It makes again one's own what was once one's own because one made it. This act is not only part of the conduct of life, as James says of the act of writing itself, as I have shown. It is also an act which is enlivening and momentous. It has import, and it is life-giving. Re-reading brings about an influx of spiritual power. In that sense it is exhilarating, "infinitely interesting and amusing."

This act of re-reading is free, unbound, in the specific and again somewhat surprising sense that it is not chained by the shackles of theory. I suppose what James means by that is that what happens when he re-reads is not determined by any theoretical presuppositions about what is going to happen when he re-reads. What happens happens, when we really read, as opposed to imposing on the text assumptions about what we are going to find there. James here agrees in anticipation with what Paul de Man says about reading: "Reading is an argument . . . because it has to go against the grain of what one would want to happen in the name of what has to happen."[4] This necessity is experienced by James as freedom. It is in this sense that the experience of re-reading is like a sudden large apprehension of the Absolute. *Absolute:* the word means "unbound," "untied," "free of any shackles." The experience of re-reading as re-appropriation is like a philosophic apprehension of the Absolute in the sense that the shining expanse of matter, like fields of light or of snow, is both absolutely coercive and absolutely liberating. In the experience of re-reading as re-appropriation of the shining matter or thing freedom and necessity come together, become indistinguishable. He is coerced by what liberates him into possession of a limitless expanse, those trackless "fields of light."

What is oddest of all about James' testimony to his experience of re-reading is the relative value accorded to the two different versions of it. One might expect that the positive experience of perfect concordance would be the better of the two, since such a fit would positively ratify the previous text, as the new footprints are superimposed perfectly and easily on the old. But no, the experience of discrepancy is the exemplary and productive form of reading. Why is that? What, exactly, does this failure of fit produce? Here again are James' words, once more what I strive, for the moment, to make my law: "What indeed," asks James, "could be more delightful than to enjoy a sense of the absolute in such easy conditions? The deviations and differences might of course not have broken out at all, but from the moment they began so naturally to multiply they became, as I say, my very terms of cognition" (P, 336–337).

The experience of difference, the reader can see, is exemplary because it produces the two things especially distinguishing genuine acts of reading: pleasure and knowledge. It is pleasure and knowledge of a specific kind. Proper reading produces the pleasure of knowing the absolute or of entering into an experience of the absolute. That this is the case, however, can only be known for certain in those cases where there is deviation and difference between one set of tracks and the other. It is easy to see why. Only if there is difference and deviation is it possible to distinguish between a knowledge simply of what the text says, which is relatively without value, and a knowledge of what the text represents or allegorizes, the "thing" or "shining matter" that gives the text whatever authenticity, value, and interest it may have, a value and interest in fact "infinite." The knowledge given by reading if it is really reading is always, even the first time, a matter of re-reading or re-vision, since it is knowledge of the "thing" or "matter" on which the text is inscribed or projected.

If reading is always re-reading, re-vision, the testimony to that is the new terms, for example critical terms, in which the re-vision of the "thing" is, necessarily, now reported. Just as the proof of the validity of a given piece of primary writing is that it

is under the coercive and at the same time enfranchising law of
the "thing," so the test of the authority of any act of reading, for
example that kind of reading we call critical writing or teaching,
is not at all, as I began this chapter by assuming and have intermittently reaffirmed, that it is subject to the text as its law. No,
reading, criticism, or teaching is of no value unless it subjects itself
in its turn to the thing or matter, and makes that thing its law,
as the writer did in the first place. James, in an extraordinary
passage, says that after all he succeeded in performing that act of
revision of his novels which he had at first thought impossible. The
record of that act is nothing more or less than the prefaces themselves, that is, the "translation" of the novels into criticism. Here
is another and perhaps even more scandalous (had it not James'
authority) version of the idea that genuine reading is a kind of
misreading. The value of a reading, against all reason, lies in its
difference and deviation from the text it purports to read. For James
this is the case because the re-reader or "second reader" must
subject himself or herself to a higher law than that ascertainable
in the text, namely the law to which the text itself was first subject.
"The act of revision," says James, "the act of seeing it again,
caused whatever I looked at on any page to flower before me as
into the only terms that honourably expressed it; and the 'revised'
element in the present Edition is accordingly these terms, these
rigid conditions of re-perusal, registered; so many close notes, as
who should say, on the particular vision of the matter itself that
experience had at last made the only possible one" (P, 339).

A little later that image of "flowering," intimately connected with James' terminology of the "germ" of a story, reappears
in a description of the spontaneous necessity with which the new
term "gives itself" to the writer rather than being a matter of free
and arbitrary choice: "The term that superlatively, that finally 'ren-
ders,' is a flower that blooms by a beautiful law of its own (the
fiftieth part of a second often so sufficing it) in the very heart of
the gathered sheaf; it is *there* already, at any moment, almost before
one can either miss or suspect it—so that in short we shall never
guess, I think, the working secret of the revisionist for whom its

colour and scent stir the air but as immediately to be assimilated"
(P, 342). If we shall never guess the secret, that is not because
James has not given us as much of the secret as one person is
likely to be able to communicate to another. An example is his
account of the way the terminology of the prefaces, which has had
so determining an effect on the vocabulary of twentieth-century
criticism of fiction, was given to him not so much by the texts of
his novels as he re-read them, as by that something else which
allowed the terminology of criticism as "re-vision" to stand on the
shoulders of the terms in the novels in themselves (in James' odd
and characteristically grotesque image) in order to fly off into clearer
air, the air, no doubt, of the "Absolute" and its boundless freedom.
To re-read, says James, was to become aware, by an irresistible
necessity, "of the growth of the immense array of terms, perceptional
and expressional, that, after the fashion I have indicated, in sentence,
passage and page, simply looked over the heads of the standing
terms—or perhaps rather, like alert winged creatures, perched on
those diminished summits and aspired to a clearer air" (P, 339).

If the art of criticism is an art of growth and flowering
which becomes an art of flying, a way of doing levitation with
words, as blossom becomes butterfly, this lighter-than-air feat uses
the text it criticizes as but a mountaintop airfield from which to
take off. But if the image of flight emphasizes the element of
freedom, James always gives the last say to necessity, as in the last
word on the ethics of reading according to James I now allow him.
Here another fine grotesque image appears, mixing the image of
embroidery which has already appeared in the preface to *Roderick
Hudson* and the image of the irresistible force with which a river
in flood makes new channels for its flow. Here is another and revised
version of the image of the new footprints forced to take a new
course across the "matter" of the story: "The 'old' matter is there,
re-accepted, re-tasted, exquisitely re-assimilated and re-enjoyed—
believed in, to be brief, with the same 'old' grateful faith . . . ;
yet for due testimony, for re-assertion of value, perforating as by
some strange and fine, some latent and gathered force, a myriad
more adequate channels" (P, 339–340).

"Some latent and gathered force": it is subjection to this power, as to an implacable law, that determines both the ethics of writing and then the ethics of reading that writing. Reading is not of the text as such but of the thing that is latent and gathered within it as a force to determine in me a re-vision of what has been the latent law of the text I read. Re-seeing which is also a re-writing, that form of writing we call criticism or teaching. This re-writing, however, is not mis-reading in the sense of a wanton deviation from the text freely imposed by my subjectivity or by my private ideology or by the ideology of the community of readers to which I belong. My subjectivity, those ideologies, are more functions of the text, already inscribed within it, than anything coming in from the outside. Criticism as re-writing is truly ethical and affirm-ative, life-giving, productive, inaugural. It is a response to a cate-gorical imperative, a demand which perforates new channels, more adequate channels, in my writing, for the latent and gathered force to which I respond by way of the work I read. My writing as re-writing in its turn is performative, productive. If it has value at all it opens access for my readers and students not to the meaning of the text as such, the information it conveys, but to the "matter," "thing," or "force" latent in the work. Such a new act of language is genuinely ethical in that it fits the double definition of an ethical act with which I began. It is a response to an irresistible demand, an "I must," and it is an act which is productive, a doing which causes other things to be done in their turn. My reading makes something happen in the interpersonal, social, and political realms.

The endpoint of my exploration of the ethics of reading, for the moment at least, as I have investigated it by way of examples of writers reading themselves, is the strange and difficult notion that reading is subject not to the text as its law, but to the law to which the text is subject. This law forces the reader to betray the text or deviate from it in the act of reading it, in the name of a higher demand that can yet be reached only by way of the text. This response creates yet another text which is a new act. Its performative effect on yet other readers is of the same kind, for better or for worse, as the effect the text it reads has had on it.

Whether the reading of novels themselves by someone not their author might be another version of the same strange concept of the ethics of reading remains to be seen, though I hereby promise later on in another place to try to investigate that question. It is a promise I intend to keep.

Meanwhile, I conclude by identifying problems with the endpoint I have reached. The relation between the "matter" or "thing" and any conceivable expression of it in words, whether in the primary writing or in the re-writing as re-vision embodied in James' prefaces or in my re-vision of the re-vision here, is far from being that of direct transcription. The law is the Absolute, empty air or an undifferentiated expanse of shining snow. Though the law has force to perforate in my words more adequate channels for itself, those channels are never more than approximate. They are always subject to revision and re-vision, always "idiomatic" in the sense that they are good only for one time and place. They are never a final and definitive expression in so many words of the law as such. The text gives only itself. It hides its matter or thing as much as it reveals it. It could be said that any text falsifies or mistranslates the "thing." It is unfaithful to the thing by being what it is, just these words on the page.

The text in this specific sense is unreadable. It does not transmit its own law or make its own law legible in it. Its law cannot be read within it but remains in reserve. In the case of the paragraphs by James I have been reading, as for Eliot and Trollope too, this unreadability may be given two definitions. One is the fact that though the text is idiomatic, a particular case, subject to what James calls "a beautiful law of its own," there is an almost irresistible temptation to generalize on its basis. The critic or reader is tempted to make this one text the ground of a universal legislation for all mankind as readers, though the text neither offers nor claims any authority for that move. The text is not the law nor even the utterance of the law but an example of the productive force of the law. We respect or ought to respect not the example but the law of which it is an example, the ethical law as such.

The second form of unreadability is another form of the first. There is an almost irresistible temptation to think of the thing, matter, law, or force latent in the text as some kind of religious or metaphysical entity, the "Absolute" as transcendent spirit. There is no reason, in the sense of "ground," for doing that, rather the reverse, no reason to think we are encountering anything other than a law of language, not an ontological law, and yet the temptation to ontologize is almost irresistible. One might say that unreadability in this second aspect of it is to be defined as the impossibility of distinguishing clearly between a linguistic reading and an ontological one. What is only a linguistic necessity or imperative is infallibly misread as a transcendental one.

This is also the case with an analogous line of thought in Walter Benjamin's "Die Aufgabe des Übersetzers." I shall discuss that now as a coda, as I promised, the end beyond the end, in a final attempt to make clearer James' notion of the ethics of reading, and my own. I have already written once or twice here of James' concept of re-vision in terms of the figure of re-reading as translation. Is not James' idea similar to, perhaps a translation of or translated by, Benjamin's idea of the work of genuine translation? "It is the task of the translator," writes Benjamin, or rather writes his translator, Harry Zohn, "to release in his own language that pure language which is under the spell of another, to liberate the language imprisoned in a work in his re-creation of that work."[5] Benjamin wrote: "Jene reine Sprache, die in fremde gebannt ist, in der eigenen zu erlösen, die im Werk gefangene in der Umdichtung zu befreien, ist die Aufgabe des Übersetzers." What is the difference between these two ways of saying the same thing? And what in the world, exactly, is "that pure language" (jene reine Sprache) that is imprisoned in the text to be translated and that it is the task of the translator to liberate in the freedom of his translation or remaking (Umdichtung), since, as readers of Benjamin's essay will know, that essay is a defense of "free translation"?

I suggest that the most economical way of naming that pure language or "reine Sprache" is to call it the equivalent, the translation into another idiom, of what James means by "thing" or "matter." Benjamin's "reine Sprache" is a figure for the "thing," and figured by it. Just as James cannot name the "thing" or "matter" except in one figure or another, the figure of the blank wall, the figure of the shining field of light or of snow, so Benjamin's formulations depend at crucial places on figures, the figure of the fragmented vessel, the figure of the circle and its tangent. The "pure language" is imprisoned in the work to be translated, but it cannot be liberated by being named as such, nor by a translation the object of which is to reformulate the "sense" of the original, the "information" it conveys. No; only by a new act of language and thereby in the discrepancy between the translation and the original can the pure language, the real thing latent in both, be liberated. Both original and translation are inadequate translations of an original which can never be given as such, just as the law as such can never be formulated in so many words, in any language. Though both the original text and the law as such are matters of language, things of language, both are pure language in the sense that a shining expanse of snow is without tracks or differentiating marks. Here is Benjamin's formulation of this paradox of a wordless word. This paradox has been encountered over and over in different forms throughout all this investigation of the ethics of reading. "In this pure language," says Benjamin, "—which no longer means or expresses anything [die nichts mehr meint und nichts mehr aus-drückt] but is, as expressionless and creative Word [sondern als ausdrucksloses und schöpferisches Wort] that which is meant in all languages [das in allen Sprachen Gemeinte ist]—all information, all sense, and all intention finally encounter a stratum in which they are destined to be extinguished" [trifft endlich alle Mitteilung, aller Sinn und alle Intention auf eine Schicht, in der sie zu erlöschen bestimmt sind] (E, 80; G, 67). The same undecidability or unread-ability encountered in the passage from James is met again here. How can one decide whether that "creative Word" is or is not the Platonic or Christian Word, the Logos, or some specifically Judaic version of the Word? The translator has chosen, by capitalizing the word *Word,* to opt for the metaphysical meaning, whereas the

German would capitalize the word *Wort* in any case. All nouns in German are capitalized, and so the original leaves the reader unable to know whether Benjamin is speaking of a fact of language or of a fact of ontology, of the word or of the Word.

Nor do the figures Benjamin uses help the reader choose certainly between the two possibilities, though all readers tend to see the interpretation of these figures as crucial to any reading of Benjamin's essay. The first figure is that of the fragments of a broken vessel: "Fragments of a vessel which are to be glued together must match one another in the smallest details," says Benjamin's translator, "although they need not be like one another" (Wie nämlich [the translator omits these words, which mean, "Just as"] Scherben eines Gefäßes, um sich zusammenfügen zu lassen, in den kleinsten Einzelheiten einander zu folgen, doch nicht so zu gleichen haben). "In the same way a translation, instead of resembling the meaning of the original, must lovingly and in detail incorporate the original's mode of signification [so muß, anstatt dem Sinn des Originals sich ähnlich zu machen, die Übersetzung liebend vielmehr und bis ins einzelne hinein dessen Art des Meinens in der eigenen Sprache sich anbilden], thus making both the original and the translation recognizable as fragments of a greater language, just as fragments are part of a vessel" [um so beide wie Scherben als Bruchstück eines Gefäßes, als Bruchstück einer größeren Sprache erkennbar zu machen] (E, 78; G, 65). This figure does not make sense as the description of a physical phenomenon, though its impossibility as literal description may be what makes it work as a figurative description of a linguistic fact, that obscure and furtive linguistic fact which both James and Benjamin, I am claiming, attempt to define in figure or in story, since it cannot be defined in any other way.

The image of the fragments of a vessel that are not like one another but fit exactly together at the break, down to the tiniest detail, would seem to correspond to a relation of translation of original in which the translation is literal and exact, matching point for point the original. But that is not at all what Benjamin seems in fact to want to say. The task of the translator is not to

produce a text in the new language which resembles the original
(which would seem to be the most obvious meaning of Benjamin's
image). Rather, the task of the translator is to incorporate in the
new language the mode of signification of the original, that is, the
way in which the original encrypts within itself that "pure language"
hidden in every valid piece of writing in any language. This is that
expressionless and creative word which is meant by all languages,
or, as Benjamin puts it in a nearby sentence, "some ultimate, decisive
element [that remains] beyond all information—quite close and yet
infinitely remote, concealed or distinguishable, fragmented or powerful" (so bleibt ihm ganz nah und doch unendlich fern, unter ihm
verborgen oder deutlicher, durch ihn gebrochen oder machtvoller
über alle Mitteilung hinaus ein Letztes, Entscheidendes) (E, 79; G,
66).

      Benjamin's image of the broken vessel does not corre-
spond to this concept of a pure language. The image does not
translate the concept. For Benjamin the translation does not carry
over the original well or badly into another language, in a relation
like that between the two adjacent and matching edges of broken
pieces of pottery. Both the original and the translation are bad
translations of a lost original, that vessel which cannot be reconstructed as such from any possible assemblage of pieces. It lies
rather both within them all as an absence and at the same time
beyond them all, quite close and yet infinitely remote. The reader
glimpses Benjamin's meaning through the discrepancy between the
image and what it is meant to convey. This is a mode of understanding strictly analogous to the way both an original and its
translation fail to express the expressionless word as such, though
the relation of discrepancy between the two liberates the pure
language which is under the spell of one or another impure language,
enchanted and masked like the handsome prince within the ugly
frog in the fairy tale. Benjamin's figure of the broken fragments
of a vessel is just such a frog. It is an impossible metaphor. It fails
to carry the meaning that is entrusted to it, since the fragments
must fit and not fit, and they must both be parts of a greater vessel
and not part of that vessel. That vessel has no shape and no

meaning, since it is the place where all information, all sense, all shape, and all intention are extinguished in the expressionless word (or Word).

Benjamin's other image is no more than another species of prince-carrying frog, another impossible metaphor. "And what of the sense in its importance for the relationship between translation and original?" asks Benjamin. "A simile may help here," he answers. "Just as a tangent touches a circle lightly and at but one point, with this touch rather than with the point setting the law according to which it is to continue on its straight path to infinity, a translation touches the original lightly and only at the infinitely small point of the sense, thereupon pursuing its own course according to the laws of fidelity in the freedom of linguistic flux" (Was hiernach für das Verhältnis von Übersetzung und Original an Bedeutung dem Sinn verbleibt, läßt sich in einen Vergleich fassen. Wie die Tangente den Kreis flüchtig und nur in einem Punkte berührt und wie ihr wohl diese Berührung, nicht aber der Punkt, das Gesetz vorschreibt, nach dem sie weiter ins Unendliche ihre gerade Bahn zieht, so berührt die Übersetzung flüchtig und nur in dem unendlich kleinen Punkte des Sinnes das Original, um nach dem Gesetze der Treue in der Freiheit der Sprachbewegung ihre eigenste Bahn zu verfolgen) (E, 80; G, 67).

The problem with this simile is twofold. The touch is of course the point. There is no possibility of distinguishing between them, though Benjamin must do so for his simile to work. Moreover, the paradox of the tangent and the circle is that this infinitely small and singular point-touch must at the same time contain in itself a curve, the curve in fact of the circle or of all circles whose centers make a line at right angles to the tangent. The translation, so to speak, is governed by the whole shape of the original, as the tangent is determined by the whole shape and location of the circle. But that is just what Benjamin does not want to say. Moreover, though the tangent pursues its course to infinity in both directions, strictly governed by the circle of which it is the tangent, Benjamin seems, according to the surrounding sentences about the pure language and the expressionless word, to want to say that the translation as tangential line is governed not so much by the circle as the original of which it is the translation, as by that pure expressionless word which sets the law for both circle and tangent, both original and translation. That law can never be expressed in so many words. It rather leads the one who attempts to possess and express it, such as all the protagonists of this book, from Kant to Benjamin, to write something in one way or another like what Benjamin says Hölderlin's translations of Sophocles are like. In them, says Benjamin, "meaning plunges from abyss to abyss until it threatens to become lost in the bottomless depths of language" (In ihnen stürzt der Sinn von Abgrund zu Abgrund, bis er droht, in bodenlosen Sprachtiefen sich zu verlieren.) (E, 82; G, 69).

I remain with Benjamin at the end where and as I was at the beginning of this book and where and as I have remained with Kant, Kafka, de Man, Eliot, Trollope, and James. I still stand before the law of the ethics of reading, subject to it, compelled by it, persuaded of its existence and sovereignty by what happens to me when I read. What happens is the experience of an "I must" that is always the same but always different, unique, idiomatic. I remain eager to obey the law of reading but without direct access to it. I am unable to write it down or to cite it as a "written ascertainable law." I am only able to tell stories about it. I am unable, finally, to know whether in this experience I am subject to a linguistic necessity or to an ontological one. Or, rather, I am unable to avoid making the linguistic mistake of responding to a necessity of language as if it had ontological force and authority. I remain forced to postpone once more the direct confrontation of the law of the ethics of reading, unless that necessity of deferring is itself the law to which I am subject. In order to test that possibility it will be necessary to read novels and tales by Eliot, Trollope, James, and others, perhaps Kleist, Hawthorne, Melville, Hardy, or Blanchot, for example. To that task I now turn, but in another time and place, within the covers, under the cover, of another book.

Notes

1. Reading Doing Reading

1. See *The Politics of Interpretation,* W. J. T. Mitchell, ed. (Chicago and London: University of Chicago Press, 1983).

2. See "The Search for Grounds in Literary Study," *Rhetoric and Form: Deconstruction at Yale,* Robert Con Davis and Ronald Schleifer, eds. (Norman: University of Oklahoma Press, 1985), pp. 19–36.

3. V. N. Volosinov, *Marxism and the Philosophy of Language,* Ladislav Matejka and I. R. Titunik, trs. (New York: Seminar Press, 1973), p. 471.

4. For "generate history" see Paul de Man, "Promises *(Social Contract),"* *Allegories of Reading* (New Haven and London: Yale University Press, 1979), p. 277. For the phrase "the materiality of actual history," see Paul de Man, "Anthropomorphism and Trope in the Lyric," *The Rhetoric of Romanticism* (New York: Columbia University Press, 1984), p. 262.

5. I have made a start with this in an essay forthcoming entitled, "Is There an Ethics of Reading?" by way of a reading of Henry James' *What Maisie Knew.* This present book concentrates on the "fourth" ethical moment, that of the reader, as it is exemplified by the author's testimony about the first ethical moment made in the course of a re-reading of his or her own work.

6. See Walter Jackson Bate, "The Crisis in English Studies," *Harvard Magazine* (1982), 85(12):46–53; René Wellek, "Destroying Literary Studies," *The New Criterion* (December 1983), pp. 1–8. See also, for a reasoned response to Bate's essay, Paul de Man, "The Return to Philology," *The Times Literary Supplement,* (Friday, December 10, 1982), pp. 1355–1356; and for nihilism as manifested by these conservative attacks on "deconstruction," see Jacques Derrida, "The Principle

of Reason: The University in the Eyes of Its Pupils," Catherine Porter and Edward
P. Morris, trs. *diacritics* (Fall 1983), 13(3):3–20, esp. p. 15.

7. See Friedrich Nietzsche, "Aus dem Nachlaß der Achtzigerjahre,"
Werke in Drei Bänden, Karl Schlecta, ed. (Munich: Carl Hanser Verlag, 1966),
3:415–925. For an English translation of fragments having especially to do with
nihilism, see "Book One: European Nihilism," *The Will to Power,* Walter Kaufmann
and R. J. Hollingdale, trs. (New York: Vintage Books, 1968), pp. 7–82. See also
Martin Heidegger's commentary on this aspect of Nietzsche's thought in his *Nietzsche*
(Pfullingen: Günther Neske Verlag, 1961), 2:31–256, 335–398, and for an English
translation of the latter see Martin Heidegger, *Nietzsche, vol. 4: Nihilism,* Frank A.
Capuzzi, tr. (San Francisco: Harper and Row, 1982).

2. Reading Telling: Kant

1. A full bibliography would be extensive. As the tips of various icebergs,
one might cite the invocation of Kant at crucial places in their polemics against
literary theory by W. J. Bate and R. Wellek in the essays cited in note 6 of chapter
1 above. On the other side, there are the essays by Paul de Man on Kant written
in his last years and to be collected in the forthcoming *Aesthetic Ideology* (University
of Minnesota Press). One of these is available as "Phenomenality and Materiality in
Kant" in *Hermeneutics: Questions and Prospects,* Gary Shapiro and Alan Sica, eds.
(Amherst: University of Massachusetts Press, 1984), pp. 121–144. Within American
academic philosophy John Rawls' *A Theory of Justice* (Cambridge: Belknap Press of
Harvard University Press, 1971) is as much a response to Kant's ethical theory as
it is an attempted refutation of utilitarianism. For an authoritative recent analysis
of Kant's ethics see Onora Nell, *Acting on Principle: An Essay on Kantian Ethics*
(New York: Columbia University Press, 1975). Nell discusses Kant's example of the
man who makes a lying promise. On the continent, there is the work of Jacques
Derrida on Kant, for which see especially "Parergon," *La vérité in peinture* (Paris:
Flammarion, 1978). pp. 21–168. For French work responding more particularly to
Kant's ethical theory see Jean-François Lyotard and Jean-Loup Thébaud, *Au juste*
(Paris: Bourgois, 1979) and the book of essays by various scholars growing out of
a conference at Cerisy-la-Salle on Lyotard, *La faculté de juger* (Paris: Les éditions
de minuit, 1985).

2. Immanuel Kant, *Grundlegung zur Metaphysik der Sitten, Werkausgabe*
(Frankfurt am Main: Suhrkamp Verlag, 1982), 7:26, henceforth G; for the English
translation: *Foundations of the Metaphysics of Morals,* Lewis White Beck, tr. (In-
dianapolis: Bobbs-Merrill Educational Publishing, 1978), p. 19, henceforth E.

3. In an unpublished seminar on Kant's second critique, the *Kritik der
praktischen Vernunft,* but for an oblique distillation of the reflection on Kant's ethical
theory in that seminar see Derrida's admirable essay on Kafka's parable, *Vor dem*

Gesetz: "Préjugés, *devant la loi,*" *La faculté de juger* (Paris: Les éditions de minuit, 1985), pp. 87–139.

4. See my discussion of this image in "The Search for Grounds in Literary Study," *Rhetoric and Form: Deconstruction at Yale* (Norman: University of Oklahoma Press, 1985), p. 30.

5. Paul de Man, *Allegories of Reading* (New Haven and London: Yale University Press, 1979), pp. 276–277.

6. Friedrich Nietzsche, good if ungrateful reader of Kant, in *Zur Genealogie der Moral* makes the ability to make promises and keep them the very foundation of human (as opposed to animal) nature and of civilized society. In the second section of the second essay of *On the Genealogy of Morals* he distinguishes, however, between those men who have been coerced into being "necessary, uniform, like among like, regular, and consequently calculable" [notwendig, einförmig, gleich unter Gleichen, regelmäßig und folglich berechenbar], hence able to make promises and keep them and, on the other hand, the *"sovereign individual" [souveräne Individuum]* who can make and keep promises because he is a law unto himself and imposes on himself his own consistency through time, sustained by nothing but his own independent will: "the *sovereign individual* [is] like only to himself [nur sich selbst gleiche], liberated from morality of custom [Sittlichkeit der Sitte], autonomous and supramoral (for "autonomous" and "moral" are mutually exclusive), in short, the man who has his own independent, protracted will and the *right to make promises.*" Friedrich Nietzsche, *Werke in Drei Bänden,* Karl Schlecta, ed. (Munich: Carl Hanser Verlag, 1966), 2:800–801; *On the Genealogy of Morals,* Walter Kaufmann and R. J. Hollingdale, trs. (New York: Vintage Books, 1967), p. 59. One might express the difference between Kant and Nietzsche here by saying that it is as if Nietzsche had not only understood clearly the subversive implications of Kant's example of the man who makes a lying promise, that is, the way it goes against the concept Kant means it to exemplify, but had also gone beyond that understanding to propose a mode of making and keeping promises which would see the fulfilled promise as depending on the precarious balancing act of a willed linguistic consistency held together through time.

3. Reading Unreadability: de Man

1. *Allegories of Reading* (New Haven and London: Yale University Press, 1979), p. 206 henceforth AR.

2. "Undecidability," Robert Livingston, tr., *The Lesson of Paul de Man, Yale French Studies* (1985), 69:132.

3. In " 'Reading' Part of a Paragraph of *Allegories of Reading,*" forthcoming in *Reading Paul de Man Reading,* a volume of essays on de Man edited by Lindsay Waters.

4. Carol Jacobs, *The Dissimulating Harmony* (Baltimore and London: Johns Hopkins University Press, 1978), p. xi.

5. Franz Kafka, *The Trial*, Willa and Edwin Muir, trs. (Harmondsworth, Middlesex, UK: Penguin Books, 1953), p. 7.

6. Editions cited in chapter 2, note 2: English, p. 94; German, p. 102.

7. Franz Kafka, *The Great Wall of China* (New York: Schocken Books, 1946), p. 283.

4. Reading Writing: Eliot

1. All citations from *Adam Bede* will be from the Cabinet edition of George Eliot's works (Edinburgh and London: Blackwood [1877–1880]), henceforth *AB*. This first citation is from vol. 1, pp. 267–268. Chapter 17 is vol. 1, pp. 265–278. Citations in the rest of this chapter, unless otherwise noted, are from this chapter.

2. "Fra Lippo Lippi," ll. 295–306.

3. Ch. 10, Cabinet edition, 1:125.

4. See Immanuel Kant, *Kritik der Urteilskraft, Werkausgabe*, vol. 10 (Frankfurt am Main: Suhrkamp, 1979), especially paragraphs 46–50, pp. 241–257. For an English translation see *Critique of Judgment*, J. H. Bernard, tr. (New York: Hafner, 1951), pp. 150–164. For a discussion of these patterns of thought in Kant see Jacques Derrida, "Economimesis," *Mimesis: Desarticulations* (Paris: Aubier-Flammarion, 1975), pp. 57–93.

5. Self Reading Self: Trollope

1. Jacques Derrida, "Préjugés, *devant la loi*," *La faculté de juger* (Paris: Les Éditions de Minuit, 1985), p. 128.

2. Anthony Trollope, *An Autobiography*, World's Classics ed. (London: Oxford University Press, 1961), p. 37; henceforth A.

3. Sigmund Freud, *Introductory Lectures on Psycho-Analysis*, Lecture XXIII. In *Standard Edition of the Complete Psychological Works of Sigmund Freud*, James Strachey, ed. and tr. (London: Hogarth Press, 1953–1974), 16:376–377; henceforth cited *S.E.*

4. See for example Sigmund Freud, "Analysis Terminable and Interminable" *S.E.* 23:209–253.

5. The unsigned essay, which focuses on *Orley Farm*, is reprinted in *Trollope: The Critical Heritage*, Donald Smalley, ed. (London: Routledge and Kegan Paul; New York: Barnes and Noble, 1969), pp. 166–178. My citations are from pp. 168, 167 of this reprinting.

6. For a discussion of this aspect of Trollope's production of novels see Walter M. Kendrick, *The Novel Machine: The Theory and Fiction of Anthony Trollope* (Baltimore: Johns Hopkins University Press, 1980).

7. *The Warden,* World's Classics ed. (London: Oxford University Press, 1963), p. 264.

8. See Sigmund Freud, "Inhibitions, Symptoms and Anxiety" (1926), *S.E.* 20:90: "As soon as writing, which entails making a liquid flow out of a tube on to a piece of white paper, assumes the significance of copulation, or as soon as walking becomes a symbolic substitute for treading upon the body of mother earth, both writing and walking are stopped because they represent the performance of a forbidden sexual act."

9. *Boswell's Life of Johnson,* G. B. Hill and L. F. Powell, eds. (Oxford: Clarendon Press, 1934), 2:126.

6. Re-Reading Re-Vision: James and Benjamin

1. *Signêponge/Signsponge,* bilingual version, Richard Rand, tr. (New York: Columbia University Press, 1984), p. 53. Rand translates my citation as: "the ethical instance is at work in the body of literature" (p. 52). I could not do better, but the translation misses the force of "instance" as "forcing its way in," as though the "body" of literature had been invaded by a necessity of being ethical, whether it wishes to or not, as a virus reprograms its host cell to its own pattern. This necessity is not thematic. It is as implacably coercive in its workings within a poetry, such as Ponge's, which seems only to describe objects, pebbles or grass or the sun, as it is within stories and novels. The chapters of this book investigate some examples of that "instance" of the ethical within literature's "body."

2. My citations from the prefaces to the New York edition of James' novels are made from the recent reprint: Henry James, *The Art of the Novel: Critical Prefaces* (Boston: Northeastern University Press, 1984), henceforth P. This quotation is from page 5.

3. "The New Novel," *Literary Criticism: Essays on Literature; American Writers; English Writers* (New York: Library of America, 1984), p. 147.

4. See my discussion of this in chapter 3 of this book.

5. Walter Benjamin, "The Task of the Translator," *Illuminations,* Harry Zohn, tr. (New York: Schocken Books, 1969), p. 80. Henceforth E. For the German original, see "Die Aufgabe des Übersetzers," *Illuminationen* (Frankfurt am Main: Suhrkamp Verlag, 1969), p. 67. Henceforth G.

Index